MIMIKA COONEY

Unstick Your Mind

Shift Your Mindset, Develop Grit, & Break Barriers

Mimika Media

Unstick Your Mind: Shift your Mindset, Develop Grit & Break Barriers.

ISBN 979-8-9873949-0-8 (eBook)

ISBN 979-8-9873949-1-5 (Paperback)

ISBN 979-8-9873949-2-2 (Hardcover)

Cover Photo: Copyright © Mimika Cooney. Cover Design: 99Designs.

This book and all other materials is published by Mimika Media LLC. If you would like more information on Mimika Cooney and her ministry, or would like to purchase more materials, please visit www.MimikaCooney.com

First edition

ISBN: 979-8-9873949-1-5

This book was professionally typeset on Reedsy.
Find out more at reedsy.com

Contents

Invitation   v

Reviews   vi

Important Note   vii

I   Unstick Your Mind

1   Why Mindset Is Everything   3

2   Power of Awareness   13

3   What Is Your Stuck Story?   23

4   The Toddler, Teenager, & Therapist   31

5   Slow Down to Speed Up   38

6   The Emotional Roller Coaster   49

7   Done Is Better than Perfect   60

8   Renew Your Mind   66

9   Power of Words   77

10   Habit Reinvention   86

II   Unlock Your Mind

11   Pivot, Adapt, Opportunity   99

12   Challenging Limiting Beliefs   107

13   Stop the Self-Sabotage   115

14   Fixed versus Growth Mindset   120

15   Fixed to Flexibility   124

16   Pushing Through Boundaries   130

17   How to Develop a Resilient Mindset   136

18 Unlock Possibility Thinking   142

19 Critical Thinking   148

20 Intentional Change   155

21 Dreaming & Visioneering   165

Extra Offers   170

Notes   172

About the Author   175

Also by Mimika Cooney   177

Invitation

As a thank you for purchasing this book, I would love to gift you with the digital version of the Study Guide. Print out this extra tool to help you work through the book. Download your free gift here:

https://www.mimikacooney.com/unstick

Reviews

"This is a tour de force of how to liberate your energy and create the future you would love to be living. It is like hundreds of hours of TED talks, motivational speeches and synthesis of self-help books in an easy to read, organized dosage. Read it and hope!"
- **Richard Boyatzis**, PhD, Distinguished University Professor, Case Western Reserve University, co-author of the international bestseller, *Primal Leadership* and the new *Helping People Change*.

"Mimika offers fresh and lighthearted insight on some hard but true psychological concepts. I found her desire to apply these tools into her own everyday life along with her fierce love of scripture, a beautiful merging of two worlds. Bridging the gap of psychology and spirituality is hard enough as a professor, but Mimika has found a fresh way to lightheartedly yet fiercely call the bride of Christ to wake up and begin to think for herself, heal and overcome."
- **Dr. Beth Reiners**, PsyD, Professor at Liberty University.

Important Note

This book is written to be informational and does not constitute medical advice. The resources are provided for informational purposes only, and should not be used to replace the specialized training and professional judgment of a healthcare or a mental healthcare professional. This book merely assembles the evidence compiled and analyzed by others—principally the Bible and experts and external sources—and provides it for your assessment.

More importantly, mental health conditions are complex, people differ widely in their conditions and responses, and interactions with other conditions and treatments are best evaluated by a physical examination and consultation with a qualified clinician. The outline in this book is a good starting point to discuss potential mental health treatments with your physician or other healthcare practitioner.

Please always consult a trained mental health professional before making any decision regarding treatment of yourself or others. Self-help information and information from the this book is useful, but it is not a substitute for professional assistance. The sole purpose of this book is to offer resources and information to those dealing with mental challenges. We cannot, and will not, assume the role of your physician or therapist. Mimika Cooney does not claim to or provide mental health treatment or advice.

If you need help, please contact a Crisis Clinic or a qualified mental healthcare provider. Please seek professional help immediately:

- if you have thoughts of killing (or otherwise harming) yourself or others;
- if you are gravely disabled (unable to care for yourself);
- if you are abusing substances;
- or if you or someone else is in any danger of harm.

I

Unstick Your Mind

1

Why Mindset Is Everything

"For as he thinks in his heart, so *is* he. "Eat and drink!" he says to you, But his heart is not with you."
Proverbs 23:7, NKJV

Imagine yourself at a party where you're being blasted by this loud, booming noise. It has drowned out everything else, to the point you can't make sense of what anyone is saying. All you can focus on is the loud noise, and you hear the booming drums on repeat. If you step out of that room, and you get into a room of peace and quiet, your brain says, "Oh, finally I can hear myself think."

This is what we do to ourselves when we listen to our stuck stories of past pain. It's like being glued to the TV or social media watching the negative news. Changing your environment, your thoughts, your habits, and your beliefs is about challenging your status quo. As adults, we think who we have become is unchangeable; however, that is proving to be false. The good news is that you are not destined to live with the brain you were born with—you can change! You can achieve a renewal or 'make-over' by applying the concepts of neuroplasticity and neuroscience.

What is Neuroscience?

Neuroscience research is revealing that the brain is an amazing organ that actually does heal itself, if we allow it to heal. Neuroplasticity[1] is the ability of neural networks in the brain to change through growth and reorganization. It is when the brain is "rewired" to function in a way that differs from how it previously functioned or was taught. We do this using Metacognition, which is thinking about what we are thinking about.

According to the Merriam-Webster dictionary, Metacognition[2] is the "awareness or analysis of one's own learning or thinking processes."

Psychologists describe Metacognition[3] as "a term used to describe the act of monitoring our own thoughts. They have found that this talent or ability varies remarkably from person to person," based on our biases, beliefs, and cultural upbringing. Being aware of our own mind, how well it is operating, and what kind of biases it may have, allows us to make better decisions. This is a very useful quality to have in developing emotional intelligence.

There are more neural pathways in your brain than there are stars in the sky.

Brain Facts

Did you know that there are more neural pathways in your brain than there are stars in the sky? Just think about that. Look up at the stars at night and realize that the stars are infinite. If you just think about the enormity, and how amazing God made our brains, we haven't yet tapped into our full potential. We only use parts of it.

Your brain uses 20 percent of the oxygen in your whole body. The good news is that you can change your brain and you can age backwards according to Dr. Daniel Amen[4] . You are not your brain, and you can change the way you approach life. You can change your way of thinking, especially when you think about habits, mindsets, and programmed behaviors.

This is a good reason to ask yourself why you believe what you believe. What is your purview and your worldview? Have you considered where you learned that way of thinking? What if everything you've been taught is wrong, and what you know isn't 100 percent true?

We all believe the stories we tell ourselves, and yet we have never challenged our way of thinking. We are walking around like drones who are asleep, being tossed to and fro in life.

There is a mental shift that takes place that makes people think, "I can do this." They start believing in possibility. What we've been told is, "Oh no, you're broken. You can't do that. Shame. Stay in the corner." So you never try. But what if we took that away and just said, "There are no limitations. You can achieve whatever you want to."? This is where the Bible rings true.

"I can do all this through him who gives me strength."
Philippians 4:13, NIV

That is what it means to partner with God. He is made known and He is made strong in our weakness. It's only when we let go and say, "Okay, God, I don't know how to make this happen, but I'm going to do the things that only I can do. You've got to come to the party and do your thing," then He can respond, "Great, now we can finally do something."

Allowing yourself that mindset shift will totally transform the way that you approach life. Once you make the shift, you will no longer see yourself in a situation of lack or scarcity. You will accept God's Word as truth: "I can do all things through Christ who strengthens me." When we renew our minds daily as a lifestyle habit, it permeates every aspect of our lives.

So many of us are aimlessly going through life like bumper cars. We keep our foot on the pedal and end up bumping into walls, hitting the side rails, and bumping into each other. Eventually we run out of gas or power, and we are stuck on the track. We have no movement or momentum because more speed just meant we ran out of fuel faster. In life, we are aimlessly trying things hoping that someday success will find us. True success goes beyond positive thinking and positive affirmations and creating vision boards. They're cute, but they're not necessarily going to get you where you want to go. The real change happens with action.

"Success is the successive progression of a worthy ideal."
Earl Nightingale

Mindset Is the Driver

Did you know that your mindset is the driver of your life? I have a saying that goes, "Business problems are personal problems in disguise." If you haven't dealt with the junk in your trunk from your past, you're eventually going to wear yourself down. Either you will get stuck on the side of the road or crash and burn. Hopefully, we can help you avoid that result with these tools and actionable tips, and offer aha moments you can take note of.

I've been an entrepreneur at heart since I was a child. I was born and raised in South Africa where I was surrounded by entrepreneurs. My Greek dad was an entrepreneur my whole life, and my parents had a business working from home. It was a construction business, so our house was like a train station with all the people going in and out. To me, that is all I knew about how you do life. Always hustle, hustle, hustle. I thought that the high pressure, high-paced life was the only way I should do life, because I didn't know anything else.

When we are kids, our belief about what truth is comes through the modeled behavior we see. We get challenged and we grow and we learn things. I always say I was a perfect storm brewing. I'm one of those who will admit I'm a recovering perfectionist and a people pleaser. I want to do all the things and have my fingers in all the pies. I talk at a hundred miles an hour. I only have two gears: full blast or full stop!

Eventually I realized that pace was unsustainable. Living on adrenaline, constantly go, go, going. The rat race, running from one thing to another, never stopping to breathe. In the moment, it feels great to be producing when you're busy and you're doing stuff. Adrenaline is like your body's own numbing agent. You don't realize the damage it's doing while you're doing it. Everything feels good in the moment, and you feel invincible when you think you can do everything. But eventually, it will come to a point where your body is going to crash and burn. Unfortunately, it takes a little while to see the signs. When you get older, you realize this will not cut it. This is a danger to your health. There comes a point in our lives when we realize that the way we are living is not serving us.

In my case, I really hit the wall and crashed badly from a trifecta effect. I had a business launch that tanked, and ended up with thousands of dollars in debt, while dealing with a child in crisis. Within six weeks, my mother-in-law passed away from cancer. The stresses compounded and I felt out of control. It was like I had been carrying and carrying and carrying the stress, until eventually my body broke down. I was in denial for way too long. After years of pushing myself past exhaustion, I never gave myself a chance to stop and breathe. It might be okay when you're twenty years old and you can burn the midnight oil every night, but eventually something has to give.

Recovery after the Crash

I had a breakdown and burned out to the point where I literally couldn't get out of bed. I've never experienced that kind of physical grief where your body aches. You experience the ugly snot crying, where you literally can't hold a conversation because you are dry heaving. It was just not pretty. I got to a stage where I literally couldn't do it anymore. I realized I needed time to heal. I needed time to stop and think. So I shut my business down.

After that process, I realized I had to take care of myself. I took a year off from all my work responsibilities. I got therapy and sought a coach. That year was so transformative, taking time to do the deep inner work so I could stop repeating the patterns of the past. I realized that it would be the most important work I could do. If I wanted to help others, either avoid going through what I did or move forward, it was important I work on myself first. I had to ask myself: "Am I living the life I really want to live? Am I living on purpose and aligned with my God-given calling?"

How it works with God is He gives us the test and then we get the lesson—not the lesson, then the test. We will keep taking the test until we learn the lesson.

I had never allowed myself to stop and think about what I'm thinking about. I always felt like a victim of circumstance. I would blame the things that happened to me on outside circumstances or people. I kept believing that what I felt was real as the truth. But was it actually true? There is a difference between what feels real, and what is actually true. Our job is to discover the difference between what is truth and what are lies in this journey called life, and to decide what we choose to believe.

Hindsight Is 20/20

Having been an entrepreneur for twenty-plus years, and looking back at the business problems I experienced, there was one glaring issue that kept me stuck: I had stinking thinking! I wasn't in the right state of mind. The same patterns kept showing up again and again. With a poor self-concept, I was not aligned with right thinking. I was chasing every little squirrel and every new fad thinking, "So and so made money doing that, so I should do that too." Or, "I need to learn that because so and so is doing it." This kind of attitude gets us into this negative thought space, where we are out of tune with our actual gifts. It is like you're driving in a race on a track, and you don't stay in your lane. You get so confused and so worried about what everybody else is doing that you lose focus.

Whether it is driving a car, building a business, managing a home, or riding a horse, you will go nowhere without the right mindset. If you're watching what everybody else is doing, it will distract you. Instead, focus on your mission, your calling, your path, your gifts, your talents, and what you are meant to do.

What I tell people is this: we need to slow down to speed up. For us go-getters out there, what does it mean to slow down? There is a method to this madness. We need to apply principles through practice and repetition to make new habits, to create new neural pathways and get rid of old habits. According to Dr. Caroline Leaf[5], it actually takes a minimum of sixty-three days to change an automated habit, not just the twenty-one days we've been told. Therefore, working on your mindset consistently is key, because there really are no quick fixes!

"Your mindset matters. It affects everything—from the business and investment decisions you make, to the way you raise your children, to your stress levels and overall well-being."
Peter Diamandis

Mindset Reset

Whether you're an entrepreneur, a professional, or a stay-at-home mother, your mindset is going to drive your life. It's like being in the driver's seat behind the wheel of your vehicle. If your vehicle is working at half pace and you're running out of gas, or the head gasket is about to blow, it is time to stop. Step aside and go to the garage and do a little work under the hood. Because when you can come back refreshed, you've reset, then you can drive the race in style. This is what working on your mindset is really about.

We have two parts to our brain that I like to call "the parent" and "the child." The child is the two year old who is falling apart and freaking out. She loves to throw a hissy fit when your brain is challenged. But to be the parent and to tap into parental thinking takes a bit of work. We don't have to believe every thought that pops into our heads. Not everything that we think is true; sometimes we should challenge those thoughts. Just because our feelings feel a certain way, doesn't mean they indicate the truth of the circumstance. When you get into that parental way of thinking, you feel in control.

Getting Unstuck

Part of what I love to do is teach people this process. We take the concept of what mindset is, then we challenge our thinking and apply perseverance. This will help you become more resilient, so you do not get phased by the stresses of the world.

How do I approach a problem and think about it logically, without giving my emotions control and allowing the two year old to have a fit? How can we teach ourselves and others to take their thoughts captive?

When you think about what you're thinking about, you realize you are in more control than you originally thought. You have more agency in your life than you think you do. Blaming people and circumstances for your problems only keeps you in a victim mindset. The economy isn't it, nor is it the government, or the weather, or other people. It's your thoughts! We have to take one hundred percent responsibility for one hundred percent of our results. Then we will realize that we are in the driver's seat, and we can make choices.

Hope and Agency

A powerful indicator of a stronger outcome is looking at the factors of hope and agency. Dr. Beth Reiners, PsyD, is a Christian Clinical Psychologist and professor at Liberty University. She says that:

> Research[6] indicates that individuals with higher levels of hope are more physically healthy and less susceptible to disease, have higher levels of self-esteem, enjoy healthier relationships, and perform higher academically and athletically. Hope is the perception that goals can be met, while agency in secular terms would be the power and resources to fulfill potential.

"Hope is a better predictor of success than intelligence and innate ability alone."
Dr. Beth Reiners

There is one thing God will not mess with, and that is your free will. Why does He not come down and sort the world out? That is not how it works, because He wants us to choose the right path for ourselves. He wants us to choose to be well. He wants us to choose a different way.

Dr. Beth Reiners continues:

As believers we have agency in our authority in who we are in Christ and the resources He provides us. So looking at hope and agency through the lens as believers provides access to those who may not have considered what tools and power are available in Christ.

Once you are aware of a problem, then you can work on it. But when you're in denial, the entire world passes you by, and nothing changes.

The Butter Knife versus the Axe

Imagine yourself standing in the woods among lots of trees. You have a butter knife in your hand, and you're hacking away at all the trees, running around exhausting yourself. Then you are handed a sharp axe, and instead of trying to chop down all the trees, you stick with one tree and use the axe until the tree is cut and falls down. Then you move onto the next tree, and systematically, over time, you have cut down the negative trees. You now have an open clearing and clarity of the road ahead.

The moral of the story is that using the right tools and focusing on cutting down one tree at a time allows you to you achieve progress. Simply taking a minute to recognize what you have, and be creative and curious, can begin the process of change.

This is why multitasking is a myth. You extend a lot of energy making tiny cuts, but it achieves nothing other than some cuts and scrapes. What you need is a sharp axe that you can apply with focus and pressure, so that, with consistency, you work through the forest until the job is done.

Why It Matters

To create momentum, let's help you make small changes so you can achieve anything you want in life using a growth mindset. It's important to realize that changing how you think takes time; it won't happen overnight. It will require daily practice and repeated habits to rewire your brain into accepting new thought patterns. If you want to achieve your goals, it's important to continue to develop a growth mindset. With daily practice, you'll be more likely to overcome obstacles and reach your full potential!

Self-Reflection Exercise

- What are you thinking and feeling right now?
- What are your challenges and frustrations?
- Where do you want to be after this process?

2

Power of Awareness

"The first step toward change is awareness. The second step is acceptance."
Nathaniel Branden

Life can be much more of a fun ride when we understand that life is meant for living. After all, we are human beings, not human doings. There is no giant, ticking time bomb that will explode if we don't get it right. The hurried pace of modern living makes us feel so rushed to get things done, it's no wonder we have an epidemic of stress-related illnesses.

In this journey called life, so many people are not aware of what they're thinking. They go about their life, treating it like a car without a driver, mindlessly falling into habitual ways of doing things. Many times they blame outside circumstances, other people, or the weather for their misfortunes. Often times it comes back to childhood: what was learned in those formative years, or traumatic experiences. As adults, they have not connected the dots of why they do what they do.

God says in the Bible that we are to renew our minds daily. For most of us, we shower every day. We do that for our physical bodies, but we don't do it mentally. Renewing your mind is taking a mental shower. What if we could start to shift our thinking from only dealing with it once it becomes serious, to preempting our reactions? We can train ourselves just like an athlete to think about doing things proactively for our mental health.

I like to call these "boomerang thoughts." Everyone has those negative thoughts and responses. The instigator is what I call the "teenage drama queen." She lives in my head, and she likes to be so dramatic. When something goes wrong, she's like, "Oh my gosh, this is terrible. You're never going to get over this." The thoughts get out of control, and suddenly she's imagined the end of the world. The runaway train has left the station and is barreling toward drama town!

> "We demolish arguments and every pretension that sets itself up against the knowledge of God, and we take captive every thought to make it obedient to Christ."
> 2 Corinthians 10:5, NIV

Three-Part Being

When you are feeling oppressed, go to God the Father for help in His Word. The truth of God's Word does far more than self-soothe, it is alive and active and can help change your feelings and thoughts and actions.

We are multi-faceted beings. Our mental, spiritual, physical, and emotional parts all go together. We are made up of mind, body, soul, and spirit. Our spirit is renewed and saved at salvation, our soul (our mind, will, and emotions) is what needs to be worked on, and our body the temple is to be cared for. We can't separate the spiritual part from the mental part, or the physical part from the mental part. It all works together. Becoming curious and then creative with solutions, as well as seeking God as your source, can help enormously when something feels out of control. Taking a holistic approach is thinking about your wellness in a multi-dimensional manner.

Pick a Bible verse that you feel leads you to consider your own emotions. What helps is identifying the feelings you're having, and then recognizing the nature of our heavenly Father. Good questions to ask yourself are: How might God respond to a child He loves and cares for? How might scripture and self-care help? What helps me calm down and understand my emotions? What is the source of this trigger? What are my own perceptions and responses?

Dr. Beth Reiners explains:

> The key is that instead of avoiding your feelings, you need to feel them. I'd want to see more attunement to the underlying need of feeling safe and secure. Invite God into the process or perhaps a trusted friend. Ask yourself how might others help you in this process? What are several things you do that make you feel relaxed or calm? These are some coping questions a person could walk through to build their own coping skills as they do distress tolerance work.

Moving into accepting the uncomfortable emotion, letting go of the shame and fear, and letting love and acceptance flood your mind and heart will build your emotional mind muscle. We can all feel out of control at times. Slowing down and using these skills helps us soak in God's Word and His truth, and learning how God sees us is important. In this book we are going to dive deeper into these areas.

Limiting Beliefs

Blocks, or what we might call "limiting beliefs," are an entrenched way of thinking about yourself that you have believed to be true. A limiting belief is a belief about yourself, or the world, or your circumstance that limits you in some way. A classic example[7] is thinking, "There's no way I'm qualified to apply for this job," or "I'm too old to do that," or, "I'm never going to be good at math." Maybe someone told you a lie when you were a child, and now your assumption about math and money makes you feel fearful so you prefer to avoid it. A limiting belief stops you from reaching your true potential.

Another example: if you dream of becoming a professional athlete, but you've never put in the work to train for it, we would call that wishful thinking. Now, if you have the skills and you have the abilities, but you have a limiting belief that stops you, then we can work on it. If every time you go for a run, the first thought you have is, "I'm never going to be able to do this," this is the "I'm never" negativity that is going to hold you back. This is why I love using sports psychology, as it applies so well to everyday life. The difference between athletes and the rest of us is this. They have limiting thoughts, but they have developed a habit or practice to dispel those thoughts, so they don't derail their progress.

There is a point that happens in your mind that I like to call the "micro moments" where you make a decision. Are you going to allow this thought to limit you, or are you going to allow yourself to push through? Inherently our brain wants to keep us in comfort; everything we do is to avoid discomfort. Most people are risk-averse, but nothing grows in a comfort zone. We have to push ourselves past what is comfortable, and get into that decision-making model.

Nothing grows in a comfort zone.

The Athlete Mindset

The athlete mindset says, "No matter how I feel, I'm going to get out of bed. As much as I want to lay in bed, I'm going to put my running shoes on, and I'm going to go for a run. I know this is what is going to be better for me, even though I feel like sleeping in."

That is why awareness is so key. Unless you're aware of what's holding you back, you won't know how to fix it. Sometimes it takes a bit of digging to uncover what is holding you back. Once you know the problem areas, then you can put a plan of action into place and decide what to work on.

An example I like to use is about my own challenge of learning how to figure skate. I never learned to skate as a child; I come from a classical ballet background. Only when I was thirty-one years old did I decide to put my dream of becoming a figure skater into action. It was something I really wanted to do, so I took it up as a mental challenge. What I found as an adult was that I had to first unlearn and undo the bad habits, and then I could retrain myself through repetition and practice. I had to override my muscle memory. Every time I learned a new move, my brain would scream at me and cause me to fear falling. Adults tend to overthink everything. My coach kept saying, "Less talking, more doing." The more time I spent talking myself out of doing it, the less time I spent making progress. I had to shut up my teenage drama queen from having a hissy fit every time I breached my comfort zone walls. It took practice, repetition, and talking myself off the ledge many times to finally push through for it to feel comfortable.

Failure as Experimentation

Here is the good news. Failure isn't failure: it's experimentation. Every good invention that ever happened in the world never came from the first try. Everything that has been designed went through several rounds of experiments. The creator had to learn to try, tweak, and learn from their mistakes. If we can have the same understanding that a growth mindset means, "I might not be where I want to be, but I know I'm on my way to being where I want to be," then we can start to celebrate the wins.

Celebrate the Small Wins

There is something that we recovering perfectionists don't do very well. We're not really good at celebrating when we do something well. I'm the first to admit that as soon as I've achieved a goal, I'm on to the next thing, and I don't give myself enough credit for a job well done.

What happens in our brain when we move on so fast is that we never allow ourselves to feel the joy of completion. We have to celebrate the baby steps along the way to achievement. Unless you have a way of telling your brain you have reached your final destination, you're always going to feel like a failure. You've put all this effort into a big challenge, but your brain behaves like a kid in the car saying, "Are we there yet?" This uses up brain power, just like the swirling icon that appears on a computer searching through data. Learn to celebrate your growth along the way and find joy in each and every accomplishment.

I have a love-hate relationship with goals like resolutions. Did you know that the average amount of time someone keeps to their New Year's resolution is one week? After a week of trying, they hit an obstacle, get behind on their schedule, and then they give up. Instead of having a resolution like, "I'm going to stop smoking," or, "I'm going to lose weight," I prefer to think of it as more of a growth goal. Goals are great, but sometimes they can feel a little too fixed. If you start full of momentum and then fall behind, you may fear you can't catch up, so you just give up completely. Instead, I like to encourage people to pursue growth goals and to celebrate along the way. Think about how you can make your goals achievable. When you achieve those little goals, you create that momentum in your brain that goes, "Oh, I can totally do that." This builds confidence.

There are multiple pathways to achieve a goal. Individuals with high hope can take this to the next level. When working towards a goal, it's important to identify several paths to achieve it. Cultivating creative problem solving is healthy.

Here is the truth: life isn't a destination, it's a journey. I know it sounds totally cliche, but it's totally true. We need to celebrate each day—each day, each month, each year of growth.

The Benefit of Journaling

Metacognition is a learned skill. It is the ability to be aware of our thought processes and understand patterns behind them. Self-reflection is essential for any lasting change to occur. Emotional health requires self-awareness and the ability to manage emotions.

If you want to know what you really think, write it down. Taking the swirling and runaway thoughts from your mind and putting them to paper is a way of anchoring your brain, and slowing down the thought train. When you're typing on a computer, you are using a part of your brain that is more about getting your ideas down. But when you are writing with your hand, something magical happens in the brain that slows you down. If you remember being in elementary school, you remember that writing always feels half speed compared to what you're thinking—it's a challenge to capture your thoughts at the same time you are processing them. Whereas, when you are typing, you are already thinking of the next thing, so you're not fully processing your thoughts. If you really want to slow down and know what you're actually thinking, write it down with good old-fashioned pen and paper. That way you can force yourself to slow down.

People who experience trauma lose connection to their feelings. One of the best ways to reconnect to your feelings and your heart is to write, write, write. Don't censor or worry about your grammar; this writing is for your eyes only. Write for three or four days and then go back and read to process what you wrote. When you form a new relationship with the hurt parts of your heart and your brain, it creates the necessary space for change.

Is this true in your experience? Can you write a little bit about a recent challenge that you've had that puts this exercise into practice? Once you've gathered your notes, and you see the points you've learned, find a friend who is practicing the same things, and share your light bulb moments together—and celebrate.

When you have future challenges, you will be able to see them as learning experiences that have lasting value. Making these positive brain changes, and applying them to your inner strength, changes your brain for the better.

Tolerance Practice

According to Dr. Beth Reiners, you can regularly practice to build your tolerance skills for emotional management using these steps:

1). Identify the source of the emotion.

2). Identify the intensity on a scale of 1-10, like the feeling and intensity of being afraid or out of control.

3). Increase self-awareness through observation. Slow down and become more self-aware. Notice how you respond to the emotion, physical movements, tense areas of the body, thoughts, and actions.

4). Choose healthy alternatives and self-soothing practices.

Practices like reading God's Word for comfort helps. God is your comforter and He provides a framework for truth and reality when things feel unsteady.

"Finally, brothers and sisters, whatever is true, whatever is noble, whatever is right, whatever is pure, whatever is lovely, whatever is admirable—if anything is excellent or praiseworthy—think about such things."
Philippians 4:8, NIV

Trauma Therapy

To get unstuck you need to reach that deep, fearful part of your brain. Anxiety doesn't go away if you avoid or ignore it. Distress tolerance helps, and journaling is a great way to uncover and allow unwanted feelings to be felt. Inner healing prayer sessions, brain spotting, internal family systems therapy, EMDR, expressive and creative therapies like dance, music, or art are very helpful.

Dr. Beth Reiners explains:

> Sometimes we can neglect our emotions so much and for so long, that we have difficulty identifying the event that prompted our feelings. The first step is to become skilled in making this connection. Sometimes we just want to avoid or numb or pray it away. But what is important to understand is that trauma is stored in the brain.

It's healthy to have strong feelings about hard situations. What is hard, is when we are acting out from those feelings inappropriately. Individuals can benefit from trauma therapy as it helps to identify the emotions, triggers or patterns. This can be done with the help of a professional trauma specialist who will help the individual work through:
1) Identifying the source of emotion,

2) Identifying the feeling and intensity,

3) Increased self-awareness through observation and writing a detailed description.

Dr. Beth Reiners goes on to say:

> This helps build distress tolerance skills and helps you learn to feel the feelings. Then they become less intolerable, and then can help you to take steps forward toward your healing and growth. When the emotion has subsided to a more manageable level, you will have the clarity to make wise decisions. The key is identifying the source and emotion and engaging the feeling, rather than all manner of avoidance or fear based strategies that keep us stuck.

Rest and Recovery

Rest is very important too: resting the mind, resting the body. Taking some time out to figure out where you are is the first step towards getting unstuck. You can't keep your foot on the gas pedal to the point of burnout. You become useless to yourself and to everyone who depends on you. Taking the time for yourself to dig deep, to dig out the rotten roots, and to replace them with seeds of truth, love, and kindness is how you build a lovely garden.

The real story, the one we have forgotten or simply don't want to see, is the only story that can truly heal us and help us move forward. Our brain is wired for truth and reality, but when our own situation is overwhelmed with trauma, God made our brain to manage by dissociating and disconnecting. This is when it can help to look at the stories we tell ourselves with truth, reality, self-compassion, curiosity, and most of all God's love. We bring the light into the dark places in our own minds so the light can set us free!

I invite you to give yourself the time. Rest is not selfish. Self-care is not selfish. You actually need to take the time to hear what it is you're thinking. Most importantly, you need to hear what God is saying to you, so you can get in tune with His plan for your life, and so you can renew your mind.

Execution

Knowing what holds you back is 80 percent of the effort that is required to get unstuck. Once you know what to do, you can put the steps into place, and then it's just a matter of executing.

Often we are not exactly sure what the roots of our problems are. I'm a big advocate for digging into them, so we can eradicate them once and for all. Much of the time we are dealing with the fruits of these problems, like anger, irritation, and procrastination. We can't seem to figure out what keeps driving us to repeat behaviors. The good news is that in order to overcome mental blocks, number one is awareness, number two is addressing those issues, and number three is taking action and putting the pieces into place. We are going to address all three in this book.

Self-Reflection Exercise

- What is holding you back from achieving your dreams? Do you know what is it?
- Think about and write down your beliefs and values that influences your daily life (family, finances, health, relationships).
- What are truths and what are lies?

3

What Is Your Stuck Story?

*"Growth is painful. Change is painful. But, nothing is as painful as
staying stuck where you do not belong."*
N.R. Narayana Murthy

There is a saying that there are three versions of the truth: my truth, your truth, and "the" truth. How we remember and experience (both the good and the bad) is entirely based on our POV (point of view). Three people can sit at a table at a restaurant and each will have a different viewpoint. One is seated in view of the kitchen, one is sitting next to the bar, and the other is facing the door. Who and what each of them sees is entirely based on what comes into their viewpoint. It is the same with our memories, especially when an emotion is connected to that memory. We remember things connected to how we felt in that moment, and often that feeling was determined by circumstances out of our control.

This is especially true of our childhood memories. Looking back at my own childhood memories, I've had to work through them with my adult viewpoint and rewire the truth of the situation. We may have decided as a five year old that when Dad was yelling, it meant something about our self-worth, when in fact it had nothing to do with us at all. Telling our scared five-year-old self, "You're going to be okay," is an important part of our emotional, mental, and spiritual development.

Paying attention to the needs that went unmet as a child is helpful to meet those needs in healthy ways now as an adult. Many adults prefer not to dig up the past to process old wounds, memories, and experiences for fear they will experience those feelings all over again. In terms of trauma, that would be true; a truly traumatized person experiences the trauma twice: the original trauma, and once again when they have to go back and process the experience again.

Dr. Beth Reiners explains:

> Recognize the importance of looking at early childhood wounds and pain and working through them in order to heal and experience healthy growth in the present. Moving past fear and shame is important. Christian especially can feel that they are not a good Christian or dishonoring parents for doing this. It is in a safe environment where we can attune to the heart and needs and allow them to grieve and have a witness to the pain and hurt. This is how they begin to heal.

Note: If you're experiencing the signs of trauma, it's important to reach out for help from a medical practitioner, therapist, or counselor to help you move past the pain of the past. What I'm focusing on in this book is how to help you become the best version of yourself, by using coaching techniques to help you rewire your brain by helping you to look to the future.

Flip the Script

What keeps people stuck? Our limiting stories of the past can often be sad tales. But what if we could flip the script and write a new optimistic story? Dr. Joan Borysenko is a Harvard Medical School trained cell biologist, licensed psychologist, and leading expert on stress, spirituality, and the mind/body connection. She says our biggest blockage to change is the limiting stories we tell ourselves. How we process our stories and how we move past them is how we rewire our "stuck story."

People keep rehearsing their trauma stories like a retro TV show on rerun. They keep hitting rewind on the tape, and pause on the "I'm not good enough" scene. The constant voice-over narrator keeps repeating the same lines that keep the viewer boxed in. This develops brain patterns of repeating behaviors, because we keep practicing the lines over and over, never releasing our thumb from the rewind button.

Malcolm Gladwell's book *Outliers: The Story of Success*[8] introduced the concept of the "10, 000-Hour Rule." The theory is that it takes 10,000 hours[9] to become really good at anything. Most of us have accumulated way more than 10,000 hours rehearsing our difficult stories to ourselves and to others.

The two biggest genres of limiting drama stories people find the most popular are clustered around regrets and resentments. The most underrated tool for overcoming both regret and resentment is forgiveness.

In Christian Psychology we look a lot at forgiveness and see that the literature supports the effectiveness of this tool. The choice to forgive releases us from the negative body, soul and spirit connection with those who have wronged us. Forgiveness is an act of kindness to ourselves, not just to the person who has hurt us. Forgiveness begins the process of healing the wounds and replacing the lies with truth.

> "Whoever conceals their sins does not prosper, but the one who
> confesses and renounces them finds mercy."
> Proverbs 28:13, NIV

Forgiveness

The key to cleanse yourself of a toxic story is to process compassionate forgiveness toward yourself and for others. Forgiveness training does not come naturally to most people, but it can be taught. Your brain, body, and soul want to cling to the story, because in some weird way, it has become part of your identity. To break the toxic cycle, you have to move through forgiveness to find relief and release. When you are not willing to forgive other people, you assume the role of victim. Victimhood garners attention and pity, which is a form of negative attention. When we become addicted to the attention that our stuck stories attract, it can be hard to let them go. When you develop enough awareness, you realize that nobody enjoys hearing your woeful tales of toxicity and drama. Living in a primordial rut of regret and resentment is not living in the love, joy, or peace that God promises us.

Pattern Interrupt

To reframe your frame of reference, you have to start telling yourself another story. This is a form of narrative medicine. Once you are sick and tired of how your stuck story is limiting you, then you are ready to change and create a new story. You're able to get unstuck through your motivation to change. You gather the power to change the frame of reference of your current reality.

Think about how you can spark a whole new way of approaching the problem. Can you be open to seeing your story from another viewpoint? What if you were not in the starring role of the movie of your life, but instead were the viewer or observer? What if you could watch the scene from your life through the eyes of someone else who is more objective?

The first step toward change is about changing recurring patterns. If you can get your brain to grasp an alternative reality, a different viewpoint, another story line, then you can make change happen.

Unmet Needs and Expectations

"We lock into patterns and try to take care of ourselves in ways that aren't so adaptive."
Dr. Tara Brach

Throughout life we are seeking to have our needs met. Newborn babies are born helpless, and their crying gets frazzled parents to respond to their needs. As we grow, we still have needs centered around safety, getting rewards, love, respect, nourishment, and connection. When our needs go unmet, this results in us taking care of ourselves, and we get stuck in patterns that are not always so adaptive. What served us well as a newborn infant will not serve us as a functional adult. The problem lies in that the brain is always seeking comfort. It prefers reliable forms of habits, behaviors, and patterns to get what it wants. If something had worked in the past, the brain likes to keep repeating that pattern again and again. We learn ways to go after what we want, and then we get identified without habits and patterns of protecting and defending ourselves. Along the journey of life, we forget who is the real person behind the mask.

Neurons that fire together wire together.

In neuropsychology there is a viewpoint that says, "Neurons that fire together wire together." The neural pathways in the brain adapt to patterns, just like driving on a pathway on a dirt road. At first it is hard to see where the road will lead. But the more the road is used, the easier it is to see the tire tracks, and it follows the path of least resistance. If you are more adaptive, then you will be open to try different things. The more aware you are of the roads or thought patterns, the easier it is to recognize when the path you are on is no longer serving you. If you can recognize a stuck pattern, and allow the friction and discomfort of that "stuckness" be a wakeup call, then you will have the resilience and creativity to get unstuck. See the discomfort as a neon sign that it is time to be open to try something new.

Recreating a new pattern or making new pathways means changing the response to the stimulus and finding new ways to cope that lead to healthier outcomes. It does take time and practice but it is worth the effort and energy.

Self-Judgment

As humans we judge ourselves for being stuck. We don't like who we are when we are out of control. This leads to feelings of shame. The first thing about getting unstuck is to forgive the "stuckness." We will remain imprisoned if we layer in shaming. If you are stuck in procrastination, you are also embarrassed and ashamed that you don't have it all together. You're not being who you really want to be, so you end up sabotaging yourself. Am I right?

The first step is to forgive the fact that you're stuck. If you can acknowledge where that stuckness is coming from (which is usually fear or self-doubt), then you can apply self-compassion. Be willing to dig deep to underneath the real unmet need. What is the want or the fear that is driving the thought and behavior that is keeping you in the stuck cycle? When you can be honest and vulnerable with yourself and show yourself some kindness, change can begin. Be willing to investigate what is underneath your behaviors to get to the root of the problem. Ask yourself questions like, "What is really going on?" and, "Why do I get so upset or triggered?"

For example, say you were bullied as a child. Now you have a defense mechanism that shows up as aggressive behavior whenever you feel threatened. The true reason why you are aggressive is not because that person said something offensive; rather, you are protecting your feelings. You don't want to appear weak or vulnerable, so the pattern is to raise your stainless steel walls and go on the attack. We react in the heat of the moment when the toddler brain shows up, and then thinking about it later we might regret our actions. If you can become aware of the triggers that set off the toddler brain, you can go back to the younger you and show yourself compassion and forgiveness. When you're not afraid, you can relate to people differently. When your brain is geared to being scared that somebody is going to hurt you, you are always on the defensive. But once you feel safe inside, you can approach people differently.

Levels of Being Stuck

There are different levels of being stuck. If there has been trauma in your nervous system, that stuck place is coming from a very deep and vulnerable place. The good news is that change is entirely possible due to neuroplasticity. Science is giving us reason to hope for healing from all levels of woundedness, because it is possible to change. Science shows how the function and structure of our brain changes dramatically if you learn to pause and name what is going on. There is a study from UCLA[10] that shows how putting feelings into words by just naming anger or fear creates a shift in the brain. There is a reduction of activity in the limbic system, and there is an increased level of activity in the prefrontal cortex. This means a better sense of well-being, balance, and executive function. Verbalizing our feelings makes us feel better and helps us to think more clearly, find more clarity, and develop our capacity to make different choices.

Dr. Kelly McGonigal, health psychologist and lecturer at Stanford University, says, "People get really confused around self-criticism because it can be self-motivating. It seems the harder you are on yourself, the more desperately you wish you could change." There is a difference between the desire to change and the ability or the strength to change. That energy is more like a straitjacket that actually makes movement and change very difficult. The harder you are on yourself, and stronger your desire to want a different life, that energy is the same energy as the energy of actual change. Dr. Kristin Neff conducted a study on self-compassion[11]. The data showed that if you can forgive yourself, you're much more likely to get back on the horse, than if you keep up with the self-criticism. Self-forgiveness acts as a better motivator than self-criticism. Pay attention to the difference between the desire to change, and how that self-criticism strengthens or weakens your ability to take action.

> *"Grieve, mourn and wail. Change your laughter to mourning and your*
> *joy to gloom."*
> James 4:9, NIV

Inner Healing Exercise

Inviting God into this compassion practice is the best way to allow your heart to truly heal. In coaching my clients, I have used inner healing techniques like this contemplative prayer exercise. You can do this with a trusted friend, counselor, or coach to help guide and support you. It starts with taking time to invite the Holy Spirit into the room and asking Him to reveal the roots that need digging up. You will have pictures and memories pop up in your mind that are a great indication of the root story. If it was a dramatic event from your childhood, try switching viewpoints from the scared child to the adult. Think of it like you're watching this scene in the movie of your life, but instead of being in the movie, you're now spectating. Engage your senses and describe what you see, hear, feel, taste, and touch. Once you are comfortable, ask, "Where is Jesus in the room?" He will show up in that memory, and you can invite Him to sit with you, hold your hand, or hug you. As the scene unfolds and the familiar feelings rise up, you can ask Jesus to heal those wounds and remove the arrows that hurt those vulnerable places in your heart. Take your time; you can repeat this process as many times as you feel necessary to remove each and every barb. Sometimes it could be an arrow of fear, or disappointment, or rage, or rejection. Allow Jesus to touch your heart and willingly give them over to Him. Once you have handed over the hurts, know that they are no longer yours to keep. You are finally set free! Give thanks and pray the blood of Jesus over yourself, and allow the healing balm of heaven to envelope you like liquid love. The healing compassion exercise may need to be revisited many times with intention and compassion. So be patient with yourself; growth is a process, and it takes time.

Self-Reflection Exercise

- What means the most to you?
- What makes you feel fully alive?
- How can you find more enjoyment from whatever brings you joy?

4

The Toddler, Teenager, & Therapist

"The toddler must say no in order to find out who she is. The adolescent says no to assert who she is not."
Louise J. Kaplan

When my eldest child was two years old, my husband and I emigrated from South Africa to England. At the time I was also four months pregnant with my second child. Adjusting to a new country, culture, and climate proved to be very taxing on us both mentally and physically. To escape the dreary English winters, we would take our daughter out for walks in the park to feed the wild horses. On the days it would pour with rain, I was reduced to finding some sort of distraction indoors. I thought I could get two tasks done at once by grocery shopping and using it for her entertainment. However, I soon learned what a mistake that would be.

At first she behaved impeccably sitting sweetly in the shopping cart seat. The problem arose when we went past the candy aisle. She knew what treats were down that happy little lane, and even at two years old she was a smart cookie. She knew that if she acted sweet and calm to get me there, I would oblige for her enjoyment. However, when it was time to check out, she would get more vocal and demand to keep the candy. The more I said no, the louder and more out of control she got. At one point she was kicking up such a fuss,

I took her out the cart and put her on the floor. She proceeded to roll around like a fish out of water, creating a huge scene. To say I was embarrassed was an understatement! The judgmental looks I got from passersby made me want to hide inside the freezers.

The first time it happened, I was so flustered, I gave in and let her have her way. Immediately she stopped crying, and the drama subsided. For those that know my headstrong daughter, if you let her get away with it once, you were in for the high jump! The next time we went to the same shop she knew the drill, but this time I was wiser. As soon as we got inside I distracted her with a toy I brought out of my bag. She held onto that toy like it was Christmas Day. I mixed up the route around the store, and we avoided the candy aisle completely. By the time checkout came, she had completely forgotten about the candy because she was fixated on her new lovely toy that brought her so much joy. This experience made me realize the importance of planning ahead, redirection, avoiding triggers, and keeping calm, cool, and collected under pressure.

"The mature person meets the demands of life, while the immature person demands that life meet her demands."
Henry Cloud

This brings me to the point of addressing the different modes of our thinking. I like to explain it in terms of the acronym I've coined called the "Triple T Thought Train." We have three parts to our brain: the toddler, the teenager, and the therapist. Some like to refer to these as states, egos, micro-personalities, or traits.

The Toddler

This part of our brain is fully formed at birth. It functions from the amygdala, which is the key structure that triggers a freeze, fight, or flight response. It gets overwhelmed easily, because it can't handle too much input. When it experiences resistance to its neediness and has information overload, the body needs to shut down to reboot. Parents of toddlers will attest to how you can't reason with a toddler having a full-blown tantrum! This mode is very uncomfortable to be in. Just like a stroppy toddler who has had their lollipop taken away, it has hissy fits, it has a short fuse, a tiny attention span, gets tired easily, and exhibits hangry like it's a full-time job. Some like to refer to it as the reptilian brain, which is useful for our survival as a species. However, this mode is not productive for us twenty-first century humans. The toddler suffers from problems when there is a lack of attachment, or when you feel unloved, or rejected.

The Teenager

Like most teens on this thought train, it does not like being told what to do. It struggles with completing tasks, repeats, "I'm bored," and moves on to the next thing without pushing through the hard stuff. In this mode, we use our dopamine system to escape the toddler to get things we think will make us feel better. We chase rewards, use addictions to escape reality, and chase immediate gratification. It does things that make the ego feel good, but are not necessarily the answer to real happiness. Like most teens, it has an intense fear of missing out and is stuck in the comparison trap, thinking it has less than others. The teenager is lazy, procrastinates, is rebellious, prefers quick fixes, and lives on an emotional roller coaster. The teenager has a lack of emotional intelligence and awareness and lives in the "me, me, me" train station. It is a confusing state to be in, because just like pubescent hormones, it is driven by primal urges to chase status, popularity, or immediate gratification. The downside is once you get them, often your dopamine system adjusts, so you feel empty again, and the cycle continues. After a certain amount of time, it gets bored and is on to chase something else. This mode of thinking drives consumerism, which compels people to keep upgrading their phone, their car, and sometimes their husband or wife! Economists call this the "hedonic treadmill" or "hedonic adaption," terms which were coined by Philip Brickman and Donald T. Campbell in 1971[12]. Marketers know how to manipulate consumer behavior using the hedonic treadmill. Most people get stuck on the roller coaster ride between the toddler and the teenager, because these are unconscious states of mind.

The Therapist

The adult train prefers a leisurely five-star travel experience with concierge service. The therapist does not allow the frenzied toddler or teenager to rush it or to cause panic. It knows how to slow down, embraces logical thinking, and is patient. The therapist's job is to discipline the toddler and teenager. It does this by becoming more conscious of triggers, hot buttons, and situations to avoid. This thought train allows us to improve our well-being by mastering our urges and impulses. It's tied to the prefrontal cortex in our brain, which is our ability for executive functioning. The therapist sees the bigger picture, takes the long-term view, and transmits inner wisdom. It functions with compassion and joy, rather than with haphazard emotional responses or the social conditioning that the mindless toddler and teenager live in.

Just by being aware of when you're in the toddler brain and when you're in the teenage brain, and being able to name your thought mode will turn on your adult therapist brain. Slowing things down and thinking like a therapist is the key, so you don't mindlessly continue acting out as a misbehaving toddler or teen.

How do we do this? You assess your "Mental Maturity Meter" (MMM) by taking your "Thought Thermometer" (TT) and measuring your "Emotional Equilibrium" (EE). I love acronyms and alliterations, can you tell?

Recognizing what state your mind is in will help you bring you back to your senses. Exercising self-control by recognizing bad thoughts patterns, triggers, and hot buttons makes you a confident therapist.

Dr. Beth Reiners says:

> Emotional regulation and self soothing can help calm difficult emotions and lead to greater feelings of self efficacy. Having feelings

is healthy and human. It's that we understand how to regulate them and cope in order to adjust and move through our lives with confidence and clarity. Sometimes there is ambiguity and self-compassion is important.

Dr. Brene Brown[13] illustrates through her shame research that we need to own our story and embrace our vulnerabilities. Only when we are brave enough to explore the darkness will we discover the infinite power of our light.

Cultivate Curiosity

The key to being able to switch your thought mode is to cultivate curiosity. Asking yourself, "Why am I thinking or feeling this way?" will open your mind to possibility thinking. This way you will think clearly and can explore creative thinking by taking charge of the unruly toddler and teenager who are out to ruin your day.

We all experience challenges and hardships in life, but we need to stop calling our responses to them a "mental health" problem. It is not a mental problem, but an emotional maturity problem! We have not been taught how to regulate our emotions, how to differentiate between thoughts and emotions, and how to work through them.

People often label things like depression, anxiety, and fear as "mental health," when in fact they are emotional responses. Labeling yourself and owning terms like "my anxiety" or "my depression" is like wearing a heavy coat that keeps you weighed down and in bondage. Believing that you are broken and doomed to a lifetime of mental woes is the root of the problem!

> *"This means that anyone who belongs to Christ has become a new person. The old life is gone; a new life has begun!"*
> 2 Corinthians 5:17, NLT

We have mislabeled "mental health" issues when, in fact, there is a major difference between mental health and emotional health. A true mental health condition, for example, like schizophrenia, is debilitating. The individual cannot function like a normal human. Often this is because of an internal mental processing and wiring problem that requires psychiatric help, medication, and treatment.

As a society, we have become too flippant about the term "mental health" and use it as a colloquial term. The same goes for the word "trauma." It is not cool to refer to something trivial as traumatic when, in fact, an individual who has experienced true levels of trauma feels debilitated. Not getting likes on Instagram is not "traumatic." Let's get clear on the differences between trauma and trials: the challenges in life we experience are supposed to help us navigate life lessons to build our character. Not everything negative is traumatic, and even experiencing something traumatic does not mean you are stuck in that state forever. The good news is that you can change your brain to change your life! Stay curious, not critical, and be ready to ask yourself "Why?" to open up your mind to possibilities.

Triggers and Hot Buttons

As we process through each stage of the "Mental Maturity Meter," we can move up the levels so we are better equipped to handle more challenging skills.

Toddler Triggers

Change or disruption to routine, feelings of not being safe, lack of stability and security. Uncertainty and threat of negative future outcome. Feeling powerless, overwhelmed, and out of control. Fears isolation, rejection, and social stigma. Focused on self-preservation.

Teenager Triggers

Seeks reward (money, status, validation, safety, comfort), relief from negative feelings (using addictions, distractions, delays). Strong urge to control experiences and outcomes. Risk-taker that believes high-stake rewards are worth it. Tunnel vision and strong attachment to a desired outcome. Dramatic responses to life challenges as being catastrophic or unbearable. Focused on chasing rewards and have a fear of missing out (FOMO).

A good way to know what brain thought mode you are in is to ask yourself these questions:

- What situation triggers this state of mind?
- How does my body feel in this state of mind?
- What is the voice in my head saying in this state of mind?

Remember, awareness is key. When you are aware of what triggers your thoughts and behavior, then you can act on changing it. What events, actions, feelings and thoughts do you notice? When you recognize the beliefs that produce or reinforce the feelings of shame, for example, it's important to challenge the belief. You can do this with a trusted friend or loved one, or consider how your heavenly Father thinks of you. If you have a healthy God image and recognize His depth of love and affection towards His children, you can accept His healing.

Self-Reflection Exercise

- What are you sensing from your sub conscious mind that you've become aware of that upsets you and others?
- What habits are you acting out when you feel anxious, worried, rushed, stressed, angry, emotional, or triggered?
- What is the common denominator that messes up your relationships?
- What are your triggers?

5

Slow Down to Speed Up

"Slow and steady wins the race."
Robert Lloyd

You're in the car driving on the highway, and you see signs flash past you. If you're going one hundred miles an hour, you're going to miss the exit. When you miss the exit, you miss out on the refreshment stations and rest areas. Without proper rest, refueling, and recovery, your car isn't going to take you the full distance. If you apply less speed and more intentionality, it's amazing how the journey becomes so much more enjoyable. When you are going at a safe speed, you can appreciate your surroundings. Suddenly you are able to admire the scenery and see things you missed. When you are not in such a busy rush to get there, you really do enjoy the journey called life. This is what I mean by slowing down to speed up.

I'm sure you've probably experienced this before, like I have, where you are driving in the car, and the next minute you find yourself at home. You have no recollection of how you got there, or what you did along the way, because you blacked out. Too many people in life wake up someday and say, "How did I get here?"

This happens in our brain when we've had too much stimulus. We cannot take in and process anymore when we experience information overload. The computer in your brain slows down and crashes when its memory is full. The only way to get it to work again at full capacity is to reboot, clear the cache, and ditch the trash that is slowing its progress.

Our brain prefers to use less energy to complete tasks, so anytime we can create a habit, we can rely on muscle memory. What we want to do is allow our brain to process effectively. This is why it's important to understand what you are thinking about. In today's age of high-speed internet, apps, software and microwaves, we've lost the art of contemplative thinking. Sometimes speed isn't going to get us there. We actually need to slow down to speed up.

How many of us will agree that we have lots of great ideas in the shower? It's because we are not thinking about the thing. We are in a relaxed state of mind, and that's when our brain is given time and space to process.

You are uniquely wonderful. No one in this world, either in the past or present, has your unique DNA, fingerprint, or life purpose. Even though we talk in generalities, you are not general; you are one-of-a-kind. You are born with a God-given purpose to serve something greater than yourself, to help others and to make a difference. Sometimes you may get stuck on the side of the road. Either you fixate on what everyone else is doing, that will slow down progress, or you get stuck in a ditch of despair. I get it; I was once there too. The key to progress is to focus on your own path and to go at your own speed. The good news is that if you keep moving forward with momentum, you will eventually reach your destination.

> "Life is one big road with lots of signs. So when you riding through the ruts, don't complicate your mind. Flee from hate, mischief and jealousy. Don't bury your thoughts, put your vision to reality. Wake up and live!"
> Bob Marley

Confession Time

I'm a recovering perfectionist. I've always been very driven, self-motivated, and a go-getter. My husband says I have two gears: full blast or full stop. I'll just keep going until I drop. In 2016 I had a tri-factor of events including a business failure, losing a close family member to cancer, and dealing with a child in crisis. I kept pushing until the wheels fell off the bus. I hit a wall big time. I fell apart physically, mentally, emotionally, and spiritually. I could not carry on. I spent three months in my pajamas feeling stuck, in despair, and disillusioned. Once I came to the end of myself, I finally realized that I had to change. I could not continue at this pace.

It got me asking some really deep questions: Why am I here? What is my purpose? Who had I become in the pursuit of perfection, people pleasing, and chasing accolades? All that achievement became empty. I needed to figure out what was going on under the hood of my car, because there was smoke billowing. It took me down to the root of studying coaching, how the brain works, and neuroscience. I wanted to know how to fix my bad habits. How do I change this behavior? What motivates me to change? What motivates my decision-making? What motivates action or inaction? How can I hack my brain to get past those limiting beliefs or restrictions I put on myself? How can I process unconscious behaviors that came from how I was raised?

Life brings daily stresses and strains. Many times there are road signs along the way that say, "Slow down, speed bump coming, road closed." For many of us driven individuals, we just keep going with our foot on the pedal until we run out of gas. Working through compassionate self-coaching, and being kind to yourself, is the key to unlocking what keeps you stuck. In my case, ever since I gave up my membership to "Control Freaks Anonymous," it's been a much more fun ride!

Trust the Process

I'm still a work in progress, but I make sure to keep the momentum of growth. I'm a woman of faith, and I strongly believe that your spiritual side is your internal compass, the real you. You have a soul, which is your mind, your will, your emotions. Then you have your body, which is your physical manifestation of your spirit on earth. I'm a firm believer that the brain can change. Neuroplasticity and modern science is finally proving this. What we've questioned and wondered about for years is finally showing to be true.

What the great philosophers, poets, prophets, and people of faith tried to argue for years is finally being embraced as truth. There is something in the cosmos that is bigger than we can fathom.

The good news is that the brain is malleable and is not fixed. No matter what brain you have, you can age backwards. Both Dr. Daniel Amen[14] and Dr. Caroline Leaf[15] have dedicated their lives' work to prove that we can change our brain to change our lives.

Having gone through the process myself, following all their processes, and learning and applying it, I have been amazed at how rewiring the brain works. I was able to reconfigure how I think, my habits, and my mindset, and it has given me a new perspective. Now my mission is to help other people get unstuck, because I know how frustrating it is feeling stuck in the rut. That's why my own title is "Personal Trainer for Your Mind." The approach I like to take is just like when you go to the gym. You're going to sweat, it's going to be a little uncomfortable and painful at times, but it's going to be worth it. We are going to celebrate every single little win, and we will throw a big party!

Meaningful connections with others helps us overcome grief, depression and sorrow. Dr. Frank McAndrew[16] wrote, "Humans are hardwired to interact with others, especially during times of stress." Healthy relationships act as a buffer. You feel a sense of safety, have a healthier immune system, lower levels of inflammation, and better hormone function. Thus, building healthier relationships and having healthier self-care can improve your overall well-being.

Hitting the Breaks on Potential

Not living up to our potential has a lot to do with our ingrained habits and our muscle memory. We have built these constructs in our minds by learning how to react to certain situations from past experience and behavior mirroring. When someone is aware that there is a problem, then they can fix it. If they're living in denial, it's really hard to take action. There is this desire within you to want to find your true north, and it is what I call "the compass pull." Whether it's questions about your purpose, your destiny, your assignment, or what you are meant to be doing in this next stage of life, the pull is a good thing. It creates this dichotomy between where you are right now and where you want to be. What I like to do is help people bridge the gap between the two. Sometimes it takes asking some hard questions and looking under the hood to reveal, "How am I thinking?"

Resistance to Change

Coming from an entrepreneurial marketing background, I was taught many hacks and tools and marketing strategies to help a business grow. I've always said that business and relationship problems are personal problems in disguise. What I discovered from coaching many people is that they don't need more hacks, they don't need more courses, they don't need more tools or strategies. What they do need is to think about what they're thinking about!

What I found was if my client kept having a fear response to change, they were hitting the brakes on growth. Those feelings of, "I could be there," and, "I should be there," and, "Why am I not there?" are frustrating. That is the loop that keeps people stuck. Eventually what happens is you either burn out or you give up. Many people just resign themselves to a mediocre life and give up on their dreams. That is a crying shame, with so much lost potential. Maybe you are not showing up fully in your business, your job, or your relationships, and you're struggling, but you can't seem to put your finger on the cause. Know that it is not your fault; it could be that your brain is putting the brakes on your potential! When we can identify the brakes, we can release them and move forward.

Denial Is No Longer an Option

Why is it important for you to change? Alcoholics Anonymous says that you have to be able to admit that you have a problem for you to work on it. Anybody who goes to rehab knows they have to admit they have a drug problem in order for them to be helped. Here is the kicker: you can't help somebody who doesn't want to be helped. They have to come to the awareness that something is wrong and admit something needs to change. They have to accept the invitation to join the party.

If we have a problem and we want to find a solution, we must be willing and open to being challenged to think in a different way. In my case, it was a giant wake-up call of hitting the burnout and breakdown wall, until I completely fell apart. I don't advise you to wait until that point. I like to encourage people to see the signs and to start to think about your life deeply now, before you crash and burn.

Risk-Taking

Many people are risk averse. Sometimes it's a personality trait; sometimes it's due to experience. It's when the fear of the unknown stops a person from doing things that are not guaranteed. If you remember being a kid, when you first learned to ride a bicycle, it was scary. You started out wobbly, you didn't have any balance, and you didn't know how to pedal and steer. You feared crashing into the wall or falling over. The good news is that you overcame that fear. Whether you had a friend or parent right behind you, they helped to hold you up until you were confident. When we achieved momentum, they let go, and before you knew it, you were riding solo. Just how learning to ride a bike is about training muscle memory, working on your mindset will yield the same results.

Run Your Own Race

We need to build mental resilience so we can recognize when things come to throw us off course. The world is not going to stop feeding the fear, and challenges are guaranteed. How do we build ourselves up to weather the storms? We need to shut out the noise. We need to calm it down. We need to go slow in order to speed up. We need to run our own race.

My husband is a runner, and he has run ten marathons in the past seven years. I'm very proud of him for finishing all ten marathons in under three hours. He is very disciplined and competitive, so he has this natural, inbuilt motivation. When he was training, he followed a deliberate training program built for him. By the time he got to the race, he had the right shoes and had done the training, so he was ready. He didn't care what other runners were doing, because he was focused on running his own race, in his own shoes, in his own time.

He is the co-founder of a SaaS (Software as a Service) software company, and they're going through tremendous growth. During the early stages of building the company, he would use the tools that he had relied on for years, like his old pair of running shoes. But with change comes growing pains. When he was scaling his company, the old tools were not working like they had before. He had to realize it was time to retire his old shoes and upgrade his tools to build a new vehicle. No longer could he walk or run; he had to learn to drive.

This is a concept many CEOs, entrepreneurs, and high performers deal with when they hit the wall of their comfort zone. The skills, tools, strategies, and habits they relied on before to bring them to this point are no longer working. They have to trade in their running shoes for a completely new vehicle that runs on fuel, not human energy. The realization is this: what got you here is not going to get you there!

What got you here is not going to get you there!

Back to the Garage

You need to get back into the garage to build a new car. First you will need to figure out how the car works. Then you need to look under the hood at the wiring. Then you need to get rid of all the old junk that is weighing you down. You might have to replace the fan belt and do an oil change and retire the tires. You can't be tinkering in the garage trying to patchwork things. You can't stick on a muffler from a Ford while you're building a Ferrari. It just doesn't work. You've got to be very clear about where you want to go.

When it comes to taking the car to the track, you will have to learn to drive. You will find yourself going so much faster, so much more efficiently, and you will use less energy. When you learn to become more efficient with your thought processes, you learn to enjoy the journey called life. You go at the speed that suits you, taking all the time you need. You remain in your lane, focused on completing your finish line, using far less energy. You will discover that you will get to your destination in comfort and style, and the journey will be so much more fun!

Women especially are very bad at comparison. I'm guilty of going through that stage of comparing myself to others in my market. When I didn't see the results I wanted, I questioned myself, asking, "What am I doing wrong?" Instead, I needed to focus on running my race in my own lane. I'm running my race at my own pace. I might need to slow down, go into the garage, and fix a few things to get rid of stuff. I need to get rid of the junk in my trunk and speed up my engine to optimize my vehicle, so that I can run the next stage far more efficiently.

Let's take away the restrictions and limitations and forget about what everyone else is doing. Let's paint a picture. If I gave you a blank canvas, paint the picture for me of how your life, your business, and your world would look. Instead of you constantly feeling like you're catching up, forget about all that. Let's just burn it all down. Let's start from scratch. Let's go back to who you are at your core.

Finding Your Purpose

The word "purpose" has become so cliché, but it's important to be aligned with who you are and who God made you to be. Being who you are not and trying to fit in is like fighting against your factory settings. Our brain is like a computer. We're constantly adding all these extra apps, and eventually what happens is it gets saturated and crashes. To unlock your true potential, you have to go back to your factory settings. Who are you? What were you designed to be?

Let's forget about trying to fix your weaknesses; let's focus on your strengths. How can we highlight those strengths? If we can do that, then you can become more confident and calm. Your thinking becomes clear, and your path becomes illuminated. You are slowing down while everyone else is at a mad rush. You are not rattled by what so-and-so is doing, because you know it's not for you. Comparison isn't a problem. Competition isn't a problem. You don't feel like you're running out of time. Coming back to your true north and who you are at your core unlocks treasures you didn't know you had.

"We know from research that growth is actually contagious, so if you want to reach your goals, you've got to get around people that are going in the same direction you want to be going, and you will catch the success."
Henry Cloud

Connection

One thing that is very strong in many countries is this tribal mentality of community support. On my Greek side of the family, there was always an auntie, or an uncle, or a cousin. Somebody you know who knows somebody who's got something, who can connect you with something. Unfortunately in modern society we've lost that. We are highly connected, but we are the most disconnected society and generation that's ever been. When was the last time you went down to your neighbor's house and had a cup of coffee and just asked how their day was? Or when was the last time you got together with a friend from school and reminisced about things?

Obviously with the world we're living in, a lot of us are isolated at home. We need to create that community feel again and get back to the basics of who we are as humans because humans need connection.

Dr. Beth Reiners:

This is pivotal to growth and health and is a biblical principal as well. Isolation breeds fear or narcissism. As a community we have to humble ourselves and realize it's okay to fail. When we work together we realize our vulnerability. Being known leads to growth and emotional health in safe spaces.

As humans we all crave a safe space, tribe, or community to feel assured that we have others who understand us. We want to open up and feel safe to share our heart so we don't feel like we are out on the fringes. We want to be in a community with others who understand us, who get us, and who are at the same level as us. So go out and find your tribe; it will be good for your mental health.

Slowing Down

This process may seem counterintuitive, but it is logical. I would encourage you to slow down to speed up. People will say: "I feel overwhelmed. I feel stuck. I feel frustrated. I'm not moving. There's no momentum." But just like when you drive a car, if you happen to get it stuck in a ditch, the worst thing you can do is apply more pressure to the pedal. You're just going to end up flinging more mud without going anywhere. What you need is a tool that is going to pull you out of the ditch, like roadside assistance. They will come and provide an extra push or some other tool to get you out of that stuck situation. Then you can work on cleaning things up in order to get momentum.

Our human tendency is to think, "Well, this isn't working, so let me try harder." As Einstein said, "Insanity is doing the same thing over and over and expecting different results."

> *"Insanity is doing the same thing over and over and expecting different results."*
> *Albert Einstein*

If we want a different result, we've got to do something differently. Pushing harder can just lead to burnout. Part of the whole process is to stop and take stock first. Figure out where you are, and then decide where you want to be. Then you can work out the steps in between to help you take those baby steps to gain momentum. Pushing harder until you reach burnout isn't exactly the best idea, either.

Dr. Beth Reiners says:

> We think that high performance optimization is the goal. But we are not Avatars we are human!

Think of how your muscles recover and get stronger as they are stretched. As believers, we need to take moments to recharge and rest. In neuropsychology it's called attuning to your heart and experiences. Instead of repressing, avoiding, or punishing yourself, slow down to allow love and healing to wash over the hurts.

Self-Reflection Exercise

- What areas of your life do you need to slow down?
- Do you repeatedly hear from others the same critique?
- Do you find yourself acting extra defensive over something you say or do?
- Is there something you keep doing but know you shouldn't, but continue to do it anyway?

6

The Emotional Roller Coaster

"People can do incredible things if you give them the right tools. It's not knowing what to do that people get stuck. They're stuck in their emotional state and they start to believe that they're stuck there."
Alan Watkins

Our culture dictates that we operate off of rules that we don't even know are there. Social rules, norms, and expected behaviors are understood but not clearly talked about. When we were living in tribes in the wild, following rules meant the difference between survival or getting eaten by hungry lions!

As we mature, our brain develops to help us continue to survive. During the preteen and teenager stages between nine and fourteen years old is when the teen realizes that something exists beyond their own identity and current reality. I've seen this with my own preteen. Suddenly she is very interested in the outside world, other cultures, different food and music.

Most parents are not thrilled about this developmental stage. Teenagers start to break the rules and push against authority. Most parents find it difficult to deal with because their once sweet child is now threatening their authority. So a battle of the wills breaks out. Having survived raising two teenagers myself (with another one on her way), I can attest to how difficult a stage this is. It is especially challenging when you are a newbie parent of a teenager, because there is no rule book to help you figure out the complexities of a teenage mind. It comes as a shock to realize that what you taught your child is suddenly being questioned. If you were raised in the old school, like pre 1980s, you probably find teenage rebellion quite offensive. How dare they question my authority! In the wild, this kind of rebellious behavior is very common, when the youngsters start pushing back against the oldsters. This is part of them learning to break away and form their own tribe.

It's actually a critical developmental stage and is not something that should be repressed or overpowered. Too many teenagers have their souls crushed when they are not given the chance to fully develop with caring support. This is something we should work with if we are to raise independent, freethinking adults with clear confidence about their identity.

We don't have to worry that they are not playing by our rules. When a child leaves home, a much bigger parent called "society" will push them back down to reality. The teenager who complains about you cleaning up his room, or doing his own laundry, suddenly becomes so grateful for your help when he has had to do it himself while living on his own. Sweet justice!

Think of the social expectations we put on our own children. We expect our children to go to school and learn to follow the rules. Then when they reach eighteen years old and finish high school, we expect them to suddenly know what they want from life. How is this possible if all they have been taught is to follow a set of rules and expectations, without any room for creative or exploratory thought? How on earth are they expected to know what career to choose that is best suited to their personality and talents, without the opportunity to learn about themselves? This is why we have an enormous problem with teenagers struggling with their identity as they search for truth. What they are really searching for is who God made them to be, and the sad thing is: they're searching in all the wrong places.

Most young adults and teenagers try to get to freethinking on their own through the questioning of authority, biases, beliefs, and traditions. This is often the stage where they question their faith too. I've seen so many instances of a once faithful child falling away from their Christian faith after their teen years, when they ask questions like, "Is God real?" The fear-based parent will quickly push them back into complying to their strict rules of belief and religion. This forces them back down into the concrete world, and they go to sleep for the rest of their lives. They are taught not to question, not to think for themselves. What a tragedy! The battle is to get them back from drone-hood so they realize that there is something else going on in the world.

The universe does not revolve around you. You are only a piece of the puzzle, but you have an important part to play. A good starting point is determining where you are by asking yourself, "What do I understand about myself? What is really going on?" You need to disrupt your view of reality to wake up your brain to start questioning what is truth and what are lies.

How Emotions are Made

Lisa Feldman Barrett[17], PhD, is among the top one percent of most-cited scientists in the world for her revolutionary research in psychology and neuroscience. She is a University Distinguished Professor of Psychology at Northeastern University and wrote the books 7½ Lessons about the Brain and How Emotions Are Made. Dr. Barrett talks about how your brain's most important job is to regulate your body systems so they are metabolically efficient. Everything from your breathing and digestion to your emotions and learning. The body is always sending sensory signals to the brain, and vice versa. Dr. Barrett says that emotions are not built into your brain from birth, but by your brain as needed and as you experience life.

The brain is fed data from the body through sensory signals using all the senses. The brain, just like a computer, is drawing on past experiences to make sense of what certain sensory conditions mean inside your body, and how it relates to the world around you. Using prior experiences to make sense of your world relates to how it conceptualizes emotion, perceptions, or beliefs. It's like an AI program that is constantly taking in data, processing it, and deciding if that data is going to be filed in the filing cabinet of your mind as a useful memory. The brain creates summaries and connections, like when something is comfortable or uncomfortable, pleasant or unpleasant. This is mood. There is a distinction between mood and emotion. The brain makes sense of the sensory changes by constructing an emotion. It creates feelings and uses them as a barometer for the state of your body. The distinction becomes really important when you're trying to figure out how to regulate your own behavior.

We all have vastly different experiences in life, from our culture and upbringing, to where we live and what we do every day. We have our own unique cache of memory stored in our brain. Emotion is variable in every human, and we are very different from each other. Therefore it does not make sense to treat situations as the same, when they're actually quite different.

Dr Lisa Bartlett [18] says, "From sensory input and past experience, your brain constructs meaning and prescribes action." Your emotions' role is to construct the meaning of a situation to help you predict and decide what action to take. What your brain does is metaphorically ask itself, "The last time I was in this situation, and my body was in this condition, what did I do, see, hear, and feel?" It begins to reassemble the experiences and make predictions about what's going to happen a minute from now. For example, a small child will quickly learn that if they touch that hot stove, they will burn their hand, so "stove" means "hot" and "pain." But as adults we know that a stove can also mean cooking, food, and sustenance.

"You don't have complete control over your emotions, but you have more control than you think you do."
Dr. Lisa Bartlett

Dr. Barlett advises seeding your brain with new predictions before the heat of the moment. For example, cultivating joy can feel hard at first, but, with practice, will become automatic. Giving your nervous system a break lets you step back from a heated situation so you can take a breath to calm your nervous system down. If you're feeling anxious, take a minute and focus on different parts of your body. Try to pick that discomfort apart so you can inject more certainty into the situation to help you feel better and more in control.

For example, when you're feeling really miserable, the first thing you have a tendency to do is eat. Some of the time when people eat, they are not eating to feel pleasure. They're eating because they're tired. Fatigue at very high intensities can feel awful. You can focus on your body, your stomach, your chest, and become more somatically aware. You may realize in certain conditions that you're not really hungry; you're actually tired. When you know you're tired, you have a bunch of different options to choose from about how to respond.

Developing the skill to pick apart your emotional reactions is a great way of building your maturity muscle. When you change your conceptualization about thoughts and feelings, you're changing the plan for action. This in turn will change your experience. A light bulb moment won't mean anything until you practice it to make it automatic.

Dr. Barlett goes on to say that our brains compute certain experiences that are in the world, and all of those perceptions are only in your brain. They're not actually in the world. We're responsible for changing our own responses and predictions to the world. Not because it's our fault what happened to us, but because we're the only ones who can make the change.

Somebody who habitually attributes their emotions to something external is playing victim and giving away their agency. You can't control other people, but you do have control over what you experience and perceive. It is very empowering to realize that sometimes you're responsible for changing a bad pattern of behavior, not because you're culpable for what is happening to you, but because you are the only one who can change it. When you accept responsibility for your own experience, it is a moment of liberation.

So what kind of a person do you want to be? What kind of experiences do you want to have in the world? What kind of impact do you want to have on other people? Once you understand a little bit about what's going on in your mind, it gives you an opportunity to seriously ask yourself what kind of a person you want to be.

Stuck State

Dr. Alan Watkins, CEO of Complete Coherence[19], says when people get stuck, they get stuck for such a long time that they start to identify with that stuck planet or place of living. People will say, "I am depressed," but that's not who they are. They are just stuck on the planet of depression. Who you are is an much larger thing than just one emotion. You're capable, with all sorts of skills and abilities. You're not completely defined by the planet or the emotional state you're stuck in. This is just like your job is what you do for a living, not who you are. Your job does not define your personality, your thoughts, your emotions, or your state of being. Who you are is so much bigger than that. Who we are is a much more beautiful, rich, and textured experience than we give ourselves credit for. Similarly, we're not just a single emotion. Part of the task in dealing with emotional problems is to try to break free from being stuck on one planet.

How Do We Become More Emotionally Mature?

We must develop the ability to regulate our own emotional state. Most human beings haven't developed this capability. Most human beings go through life not in control of their own emotions, and, worse yet, they make decisions based on how they "feel." Things like, "I don't feel motivated," or, "I'm not feeling it," have become common statements that culture has permitted as an excuse. Allowing your emotions to rule your mind is like allowing the unruly toddler or teenager to be in control. It creates unpredictability, and you get weighed down and "leak out" your emotional energy on others. Behavior like yelling, fits of anger, frustration, or mood swings are common responses to unregulated emotions. However, it's possible to finish the day with more energy than when you started, if you get good at self-regulation.

What we are not taught is how to process our emotions so we can reach the recuperation or renewal stage. We just stay stuck in an emotional state, stewing and building up negative energy. It's like being stuck in one gear, and your car is not going anywhere while you burn out the engine.

As human beings, we should be living full of passion and enthusiasm for life. When we allow ourselves to calm down from an emotional high or low and give ourselves proper recuperation time, we rebuild our emotional maturity muscle. We become more content, receptive, curious, and relaxed. So the next time things get heated up, we know how to adjust the emotional thermometer and regulate our states.

When you become emotionally mature, you understand that emotional highs mean an emotional low, and vice versa. It is in your best interest to equalize your emotional responses to avoid the high highs and the low lows. You see this with high-performing athletes, performers, and celebrities. After they achieve their goals, like, for example, winning the Olympics, things fall apart. Their whole life, up until this point, has been focused on achieving that impossible dream. Then when they finally achieve it, they slump into the depths of despair, depression, and self-doubt. They no longer have a purpose, mission, or focus to drive their daily activity. They also have lost their reason to get up in the morning. They feel lost, adrift in an ocean they are not familiar with. Inevitably, if they don't replace their mission with a new mission, they find it very hard to shift gears into being productive. We've seen this happen with celebrities, performers, and singers. They get used to the applause and adulation of their fans. When their career takes a dip, or they fall out of favor, they crash and burn. Sadly, many succumb to drug abuse, or, worse, death. It's impossible to maintain those levels of high performance without it costing something. Nothing lasts forever so it's important to shift emotions, mindsets, and behaviors to fully embrace the next stage of life.

Making the Shift

Human beings shift their emotions all the time; they just don't do it on purpose. When you move from being a victim, to owning your own emotions, you realize that you are the architect of your life. You realize and accept that nobody is doing anything to you; you are doing it to yourself. You own your emotions, and it's an absolute game changer!

The great news is that when you accept that simple truth, you own it so you can change it. If you constantly wander through life thinking somebody else owns or is in control of your emotions, then you're acting like a victim. Pointing the finger at someone else is giving up your agency, and you give up on making changes because it feels out of your control. When you're pointing a finger at someone, remember that there are three other fingers pointing back at you!

It's a necessary part of life to experience a little bit of discomfort. Only once you are uncomfortable do you have the momentum and motivation to change. Discomfort creates the evolutionary momentum to create a shift. When the discomfort causes you to change and shift, then you take action to change. You shifted your own biology and changed planets.

This is a problem amongst today's generation of helicopter parents, who try to save their children from themselves. The problem is if they steal the pain away from their child too quickly, it steals the opportunity for learning. Parents, allow your children to fail. It will be good for them!

Difference between Happiness and Joy

Happiness relies on "happenings" or circumstances out of your control. If you say, "I'm only going to be happy when I make a million dollars," there are a lot of factors that go into achieving that, that perhaps are out of your control. If you are basing your happiness on an event or a circumstance or a bank balance, you're pretty much setting yourself up for disappointment. Choosing joy is a deliberate act, whereas happiness is waiting for life to happen to you. We can't control outside circumstances or other people, so expecting other people to make you happy is setting yourself up for failure. Do you know that there are over 242 mentions of the word "joy" in the Bible?

> *Consider it pure joy, my brothers and sisters, whenever you face trials of many kinds, because you know that the testing of your faith produces perseverance. Let perseverance finish its work so that you may be mature and complete, not lacking anything.*
> *James 1:2-4, NIV*

Be joyful always, pray at all times, be thankful in all circumstances.
This is what God wants from you in your life in union with Christ Jesus.
1 Thessalonians 5:16–18, NIV

And the disciples were filled with joy and with the Holy Spirit.
Acts 13:52, NIV

You can switch your idea of success to having a sense of joy in every moment. You learn that you don't need the perfect circumstances to feel happy. The circumstances are irrelevant, because you choose to find joy in every moment.

Sheryl Lynn is the Visionary and Founder of JOYELY[20] and the *Chair of Joy*™ Experience. Sheryl has developed a metacognitive strategy that uses four principles to facilitate the science of joy. The four simple steps allow for a universal language of joy that include: sit, breathe, think and feel. You can try this super simple exercise in the comfort of your home.

1. Step one: Sit in your think chair.
2. Step two: Take a deep breath. Drop your shoulders, put your feet on the ground, and get settled in your chair of joy.
3. Step three: Think about a moment of joy as it pertains to what you want.
4. Step four: Feel it in your body. When you let that feeling of what is possible in the future come into consciousness, you feel the tingles throughout your body.

By connecting with your mind, body, spirit and soul you can make joy a daily practice. Ask yourself what sparks joy in you. Think of joy from an intrinsic perspective. If you can start to think of what brings you joy, you will start to look for it. It could be the simplest things like enjoying a nice glass of iced boba tea. Be in the moment, sense what it tastes like, feel the texture, and take in the moment of joy. Learn to intentionally shift your emotional state by becoming aware of your senses.

The Importance of Human Connection

Focusing on helping others by being part of a community will actually increase your joy and happiness, versus just focusing on yourself. Social support is the greatest predictor of happiness during periods of high stress.

Humans are made for connection. We are wired for relationships. Even though we are the most digitally connected we have ever been, yet we are the most disconnected generation of all. We feel so isolated. Being part of a community helps to clean up your mental mess when you have others you can bounce ideas off of, have conversations, who can hold a mirror up to you and say, "Actually what you're doing is not good," or, "Is this true?" Having a human connection improves your resilience, it reduces chronic pain, it lowers blood pressure, it improves your cardiovascular health. Engaging with others helps to lower your cortisol levels, increases your serotonin and dopamine, and balances brainwaves. So the truth is, connecting with a friend can make you smarter. We don't want to do damage to our brains. We want to build our brain. So phone a friend, text a friend, or go for dinner or have lunch or a coffee date. These are all great things that you can do to help yourself.

Here are some other ideas for cultivating connection. If you're feeling isolated and not getting that connection you need, join a gym or a fitness club, take up a dance or Zumba class, find a walking or running buddy (especially if you find exercise challenging and motivating yourself is very difficult). Having an accountability partner does help. Saying, "I'm going to meet you at a certain time, at a certain place," will help you get yourself moving. You could join a church group. You could volunteer at a local shelter or nonprofit. You could volunteer at your kid's school. You could organize or host a Tupperware product party. You could see a therapist or a counselor. You could partner with a weight loss accountability partner to keep yourselves moving in the same direction. You could take up an art class. You could join or start a local business club. Or you could hire a coach.

Shift Your Mindset

We need to shift your mindset. A zero-sum mindset says someone has to lose if someone else is winning. This is very toxic thinking and causes brain damage. What we need to do is shift to an abundance mindset. This means we need to reconfigure the way we look at things and realize that there's more than enough for everyone and we all are winning in our own way. What's good for one person isn't necessarily good for others. The comparison trap can be avoided. Someone else's success has no effect on mine, because what they're doing with their life is different to what I'm doing with mine. Their choices really have no bearing on what decisions I need to make for myself.

Even though it's very easy to compete with somebody else's highlight reel on Instagram or Facebook, it's important to stay focused. Realize that their success is probably due to a lot of hard work, repeated habits, and putting in work that we might not see. We need to celebrate and enhance others versus competing with them. Life is not a race, but a journey of self-discovery. We are not competing with others. We are on our own path towards success. We simply need to learn to embrace and enjoy the ride we're on.

Self-Reflection Exercise

- Decide in advance what you will tell yourself when a negative or uncomfortable emotion comes up.
- What can you do or say to make a conscious effort to shift your emotions on purpose?

7

Done Is Better than Perfect

"It always seems impossible until it's done."
Nelson Mandela

There is a secret society called "Perfectionists Anonymous." It's a group of members who don't declare their membership publicly. They secretly dislike their membership status, and they find the high standards exhausting to maintain. They like to keep up the facade that they have it all together. What a scandal it would be if anyone found out what a hot mess they really are!

I'll be the first to admit I was once a member too. I spent years chasing my tail in the hopes of achieving greatness through perfection, and I was the worst critic! The reality of living under those expectations was too much to bear. The weight eventually caused me to crash and burn. Since I gave up my membership in *Perfectionists Anonymous*, life has been so much more of a fun ride!

"Start by doing what's necessary; then do what's possible; and suddenly you are doing the impossible."
Francis of Assisi

Perfection versus Excellence

There is a difference between perfection and excellence. Perfection is all about me, and sets high—usually unachievable—standards for itself. It's worrying about what other people think, and beating yourself up when you fall short of the goal. Excellence on the other hand, is doing something with a passion and a purpose. Excellence is knowing that what you're doing is the right thing to do. As a perfectionist, I always wanted to fix things, to be in control. I was critical and judgmental of others when they didn't measure up to my high standards. The inner critic in my mind was relentless and never stopped harassing me. For years I believed the lies, and would spend days in self-pity or self-judgment if I felt like I failed.

FOMO

A lot of marketers are taught to use fear-based marketing tactics to trigger responses in people. Things like, "You better sign up before the timer runs out or you will miss out," uses intense FOMO (fear of missing out) tactics. Pressure, pressure, pressure. Using fear tactics is only going to elicit a fear response. People take action for self-preservation, and this results in buyer's remorse, regrets, and regression.

I come from a different perspective; I'm anti-mainstream. I prefer to create a safe space for you, invite you to open the door, and wait until you are ready to step in. I'm not going to push you, or cajole you, or try to scare the snot out of you either. When you're rushed and pressured, you go into desperate energy, which translates to other people and creates more of the same thing. I strongly believe in the concept of slowing down so you can make the necessary adjustments to speed up down the road. This results in longevity in your thinking, feeling, sensing, and acting. For you to enact change you have to believe that you are achieving, even in the little steps.

The Open and Closed Loop Concept

In the writing and TV world there is a form of storytelling called the "open and closed loop concept"[21]. If you have ever wondered why binging on your favorite TV show is so addictive, it is because your brain is being hacked. The story starts with some kind of conflict, or goal the characters have to achieve. Right before the end of that episode, they'll offer a short resolution. Before the episode ends, they will end with a cliffhanger. They will hype up a big conflict or question to keep you wanting more. That is why we want to keep watching.

Our brain is inherently built to find closure and solutions. It needs to come to a resolution in order for it to know that this challenge has ended, the goal has been achieved, and it's okay to move on. Our brain is built to know that there is a start and an end to things. Most people in modern society are so glued to their phones, email, and social media that they're hooked on a never-ending hyperactivity loop. There's never an off button. There's never the old-fashioned "the end" we may find in fairy tales. We don't have endings any more. Social media is designed to keep us sucked in. Whether it's Facebook or Instagram or YouTube, they want to keep you on their platform because their intention is to sell more advertising to your eyeballs. To keep you from leaving, they hack your brain to keep your fingers glued to the screen. It's like you've stuck your finger in a wall socket and are getting shocked with electricity. What's going to happen if you stay with your finger plugged in the wall? You are going to get fried. Eventually people get burnt out, over-stimulated, and they break down or shut down.

> *"Perfection has to do with the end product, but excellence has to do with the process."*
> *Jerry Moran*

When my eldest daughter finished college, we attended her graduation, which they call a "commencement." I wondered, "Why do they call it that?" But it does make sense, because a commencement is not the end of one season, but the start of something new. It marks a pivotal point in our lives where it signifies a completion of an old season, with anticipation for the new. The students who graduated the year before her, in 2020, didn't have in-person graduations. Those students may be suffering from a lack of closure. They struggle to step into their new seasons, because they didn't have a proper end to the old.

Why do we celebrate graduations, birthdays, and weddings? It's because it's a form of closure, and our brain needs closure in order to move on. Why do we have funerals? Even though the person is no longer with us, it's for us, the living, to say goodbye. It's to help us have a sense of closure and completion so we can move on. It's perfectly normal to cry sad tears and feel emotional. Just know that nothing has gone wrong; it is part of the growth process.

If you're struggling with overwhelm, one of the first things I say to people is, "What are you doing right now that you can finish and close the loop?" Stop, pause, and celebrate. Like, "Yay, I went to the gym today." Instead of beating yourself up about the days you didn't go, celebrate the days that you did. You need to build your momentum muscle. We need to make our actions and decisions work for us, not against us. This means celebrating the wins, allowing your brain to close the loop, and see closure on whatever you've started.

Growth Is Like Grieving

Growth can often feel like grieving. When you are changing and growing, you are stretching your brain into areas it hasn't been before. You are letting go of the old: the old way of thinking, the old habits, the old environment, the old relationships with yourself and with others.

When you're letting go and saying goodbye to something, it can feel sad. But a lot of the time, we don't realize that we need that closure. We need to allow ourselves to say, "Thank you. That was an experience I'm adding to my memory bank."

Why do we cry at weddings? Why do we cry at graduations? It's because we know that something is coming to an end. It's okay to cry; it's okay to be sad. It means that you're opening the loop and beginning the chapter on something new. Allowing yourself to fully process and move through the change will create an opportunity for something new.

Celebrating the Wins

I prefer the less-is-more-approach to the way I teach. You are going to aim to do one thing this week, and when you're done, we are going to throw a big party! We are going to celebrate the small things like getting your nails done, booking a vacation, writing a chapter in your book, or taking a nap. When you have not prioritized the small things like self-care, you need to rewire your mind about the importance of the little wins. We are going to help your brain close those open loops. We are going to allow your brain to slow down so it can process information. Just like having too many open tabs on your computer, you are using excessive energy constantly shifting and moving between them. The truth is that multitasking is a myth. You're not really multitasking or achieving anything; you are simply switching from one task to another. The constant start, stop, start, stop, start, stop—it's exhausting! If you're like me and love to-do lists, you feel terrible when it feels like you didn't get anything done. We just spent the day starting and restarting and never got out of the garage.

What if you switched your thinking to focus on just one thing? What if you did that one thing and then threw yourself a party? I know, it feels weird, but stay with me here. Completing the circle, ticking it off your to-do list, and celebrating the win is a huge achievement. What it is going to do for you is build your mental resilience muscle so you can take on harder things. Little by little, you are building mental stamina and strength. You keep your momentum going because you feel accomplished when you actually get stuff done.

Growth Journey

It's a growth journey. It's a process. You never arrive. None of us can call ourselves experts, because we're always learning. The goal is to help you get you back to functioning again, so you can get back on the road. The most fulfilling thing to me is seeing others go through this process, and how it helps them with their lives and their thinking. Where you'll find the greatest relief is when you understand that you don't have to be all things to all people. If you are open to allow yourself to be stretched, that is when the greatest growth happens. Is when you can be willing to leave sight of the shore to discover new horizons. As long as you remain teachable and coachable, you will find new roads and opportunities for growth. Stay curious, not critical, and you will amaze yourself at what you discover!

"For my yoke is easy and my burden is light."
Matthew 11:30, NIV

God Is Not a Hard Task master

God's approach is one of compassion and kindness, just like Jesus said in Matthew 11:30. When we can give ourselves the gift of compassion and kindness, we step into our purpose and calling. God just wants us to trust Him and take a small step of faith. It doesn't mean we get stuck in perfection paralysis because we are waiting for the perfect conditions. As a recovering perfectionist, I've had to come to acknowledge and embrace that "done is better than perfect." Give your brain the gift of done.

Self-Reflection Exercise

- What can you today to celebrate and give yourself the gift of done?
- What can you do to be kind to yourself even if you don't meet all your expectations?

8

Renew Your Mind

"Do not conform to the pattern of this world, but be transformed by the renewing of your mind. Then you will be able to test and approve what God's will is—his good, pleasing and perfect will."
Romans 12:2, NIV

Life can sometimes feel like we are living on the treadmill of just doing, doing, doing. Always feeling stressed, suffering from perfectionism and needing to please people. I never felt like I was really in control. When I found myself stuck on the side of the road with no gas in my tank, I had to admit that what I was doing in my own strength was not working. It was time to go back to the garage and figure out what was going on under the hood. I needed to ditch the junk in my trunk that was holding me down. I had to peel back the layers of bad habits and thought patterns that I thought was the way everybody lived. It was only when I was challenged in those areas that I woke up to face them.

We get an onslaught of things coming at us from the news, the media, emails, family, etc. It's more stimulation than we can handle. If we want to be on a path of where God wants us to go, we have to make the concept of renewing the mind a lifestyle habit. It's not a fad or a diet that you try for a few weeks, then go back to your old ways. It's part of a daily habit and intentional thought creation that you actively have to put effort into until it becomes muscle memory. The good news about neuroplasticity is that we can rewire our thoughts. We can change the brain we were born with. We don't have to live a life that is haphazard or directionless. We get to be in the driver's seat and change things.

The great news is that science is finally catching up with the Bible! The Bible says, "Renew your mind daily" (Romans 12:2). Just like taking a daily shower, we need to take a mental shower. Through repetition, practice, and intentionality, we can change the direction of our lives with our mind. When we align our thinking with God's Word, it's amazing how things change. It's like putting super fuel in the engine of your car. You get there so much faster, and the ride is so much more enjoyable.

The Power of Choice

The whole concept of renewing your mind starts with a choice. First, we have to be aware of what the problem is so we can fix it. If we don't have that awareness, which is the key to the ignition, we aren't going to be able to start the car. When you are stuck in park, you feel like a victim of circumstance because you're not in control. It's not God's plan for us to stay stuck; He can only use us if we are moving. Once you've made the decision to change, then you become aware of your blind spots and things you need to work on. Adopt a beginner's mindset and be open to learning new things. Be ready to challenge the things you were taught, even as a child.

God already has the tools for you; you don't have to guess. That is what is so fabulous about Christian living. God in His graciousness is not going to rip the Band-Aid off. He is going to guide you through the process and allow you to work through these things with love and compassion. The idea is that you want the change to stick, so that it is a permanent fix. You don't want this process to be a yo-yo thing that works today, but then you're back where you started tomorrow.

Renewing the mind is like building a muscle. Just like when you go to the gym, the first day feels terrible, uncomfortable, and weird. You don't have a lot of strength, and your stamina isn't great. Starting is the hardest part, but as you just keep showing up, keep putting one foot in front of the other. As you push through the hard stuff, your mind muscles get stronger.

It's the same thing with your mind. By putting these pieces into place, taking small steps of action, and repeating the process, you can rewire your mind. What are you putting in your mind? What are you watching? What are you listening to? What are the inputs? How are you connecting and refueling yourself?

God will say to me in a practical way, "Hey, it's time to turn the computer off, you're overdoing it. Time to go take a rest." And I'm like, "No, no, no, I'm fine. I'm fine. I can do this." God loves me so much that He knows when I need to take a nap, or when I should go have a bite to eat. Often it's not the epic things that make a big difference: it's the small, practical things.

Be open to change and ask yourself questions like: "What do I need to learn today? What is God trying to teach me? How do I renew this thought and change these habits so I can form new muscle memories?" Whenever you are learning a new skill, it takes a bit of time, but you can get quicker and more efficient at it. Eventually muscle memory kicks in and you don't even think about it. That is the good news. If you can be willing and open to allow God to help you work through the hard things, you will come out of it fitter, stronger, and wiser.

Taking Thoughts Captive

Change can be painful. Like going to the gym, you're going to sweat, and you're going to cry, but at the end of the day it's going to be worth it. Following the process of renewing your mind will help you feel in control of your life. You can begin making choices from a position of power, not weakness. In scripture the Apostle Paul says:

"We demolish arguments and every pretension that sets itself up against the knowledge of God, and we take captive every thought to make it obedient to Christ."
2 Corinthians 2:5, NIV

What this means is that we don't have to accept every thought as truth. We are to test our thoughts against the truth of God's Word. If we wake up and we hear a thought like, "You're so terrible, no one's going to like you today," we must test that thought against the truth of God's Word, which becomes an elixir. Let's challenge and discover the difference between the truth and the lie. God's Word says I'm loved, so that thought was a total lie.

It comes back to identity, and knowing who we are in Christ, and whose we are. We belong to the most high God, the Creator of the universe, and He says I'm loved and favored. So I'm going to reject the lie the enemy has tried to tell me. It's like learning a new language. It will take some time to learn the cadence, the tone, and the sound between my head voice, God's voice, and the enemy's voice. But with practice you'll become an expert.

A lot of us get our "who" confused with our "do." We feel like, "I'm not being effective enough," or "I'm not being kind enough", or whatever "enough." Women especially have a big problem with this whole sense of worthiness. Once we realize that we get our worthiness through Christ, through Jesus, we realize we are wearing a royal garment. It doesn't have to be about what we are made of, because God has made us new—which is great news, right? With God we are in for a complete makeover!

Choosing the new mindset and understanding your true identity in Christ can help build wholeness. It starts with an accurate understanding of who God truly is. Our past hurts and experiences can distort our understanding of how God views the believer He died for. So it is important we go back to God's Word to remind ourselves of His true nature, so we can dispel the lies we have believed about ourselves and Him.

Even if you have bad habits of thinking, you now have a tool to challenge that. When your mind is bombarded with negative thoughts, usually within the first five seconds of your waking, those thoughts will try to get you on the runaway train. You get to choose how you respond, because the one thing God will not interfere with is your free will.

Consider what happened in the garden of Eden. God gave Adam and Eve a choice, and they didn't choose very well. Let's learn from that lesson and realize that the enemy is always going to tempt us, but we have the power to choose. We get to decide every day: will we align with truth, or will we align with lies?

For me personally I had to go through this process of challenging everything that popped into my head. It was like the light bulb went on, and suddenly I started to question everything: my values, my beliefs, my ideas, the way I was raised. I would have to think about finances, money, or worth. I had to go back to see what God's Word really had to say about it. I did some research, I did some digging, I became a scriptural sleuth. I had to challenge everything and look at the evidence of what presented itself, and not just accept my predisposed ideas.

God gave us a brain so we could think. The difference between us and animals is that we get to choose, that we have reasoning. We can use our thoughts and our brain to do things that are beyond our capabilities.

Controlling Your Emotions

Emotions are part of what makes us human. In the Bible Jesus was God made flesh, and he had feelings too. He demonstrated the same emotions we feel: sadness, love, anger, hurt, grieving, joy, etc. Our emotions are signals that are part of our everyday living.

The difference between Jesus and us is that He didn't sin in His feelings, even though he still experienced them. We are not robots and that isn't how God chose to make us. The good news is Jesus as our king priest understands and comforts us in our time of weakness.

While we may think of emotions as inconsequential, they physically manifest. We feel them in our bodies, and we perceive them psychologically. An emotion is simply energy in motion. It is an energetic sense from a thought that manifests as a feeling, and a feeling that manifests as a thought. In essence, energy keeps moving, so for us to effectively process our emotions, we have to allow them to "pass through."

When you align your thinking with God's Word, you have clean thinking and a way of processing emotions. You get better at controlling your emotions, and you become objective. You don't jump to conclusions when something goes wrong, and you don't immediately jump on the toddler or teenager drama train. You are in control of your thoughts, so you don't allow your emotions to rule the day.

> *"For God did not give us a spirit of fear. He gave us a spirit of power and*
> *of love and of a good mind."*
> 2 Timothy 1:7, NLV

When you take a thought captive, you say, "I know this is an emotion and it's going to pass. I don't have to make a life-altering decision based on how I'm feeling right now. Let me go back to what God says about my identity. I'm loved, I'm worthy, I'm valuable. God loves me even though I've messed up." Showing yourself kindness and compassion is allowing the therapist in your mind to take control. We don't deny or react to the emotion; instead, we acknowledge it and allow it to pass through. This is the habit of renewing and redoing. It's not a once and done approach. It's disputing what comes into your head and asking, "What is the truth? What is a lie?" Eventually it will become natural to you, so you won't even have to think about it as it becomes mental muscle memory.

If we know that God says that He is not the source of fear, we can become aware of where the fear comes from. If you start to feel fearful, or have negative, foreboding thoughts, you can immediately adjust and say, "That's not from God, so I'm not going to accept it." We could drive through a town and not have to pick up take-out at that town; we can just drive through.

Identity in Christ

It all comes down to knowing your identity and authority in Christ. Why do you think that the enemy is trying so hard to destroy people's identities right now? Children are very impressionable and can get easily confused about truth during their formative years. The onslaught with gender identity issues we are facing is a direct attack and insult against God. We are created in God's image, and the devil hates it that we are like God. He hates it that he no longer is adored like he was in heaven and that he has been cast down.

When God formed you in your mother's womb, He already knew you and what you would become. Understanding your purpose, and confusion about your purpose and direction, is how the enemy tries to steal your destiny. So many young adults are struggling with identity, worthiness, and purpose issues because of the onslaught and attack in their minds. This is a direct attack on us knowing our identity in Christ.

Dr. Beth Reiners says:

> I think understanding that gender identify confusion can lead to more fragmentation, as we move farther away from our original design and God's intentions for us in creation. I feel at the core of our hearts, we understand as humans that we were created for more and for someone higher. What we find is that the way back to our creator can become the way back to true inner healing.

If we have had a bad example of a fatherly figure, or bad experiences in the Church, it taints our true understanding of God. Religion is what crucified Jesus! It's unfortunate that God gets a bad rap for the bad behavior of people. When we can see the greater story of a good Father that does not exploit or harm for personal gain, we can learn to trust Him.

Authority

God has given us authority, and the way I like to think about it is like opening gifts. God has all these wonderful gifts in heaven waiting to ship to us. Some we already have with us, but we have not yet learned how to open them. If we are not where He wants us to be in order to receive them, we will miss them, or they will get delayed in "customs." Maybe you are stuck on Worry Lane or Rebellion Road, instead of being at home in peace. If we are someone else, we are going to miss the package and we are going to miss the blessing. It is addressed to you; no one else has the ability to open that specific gift other than you. At the same time, there is so much more He wants to give you. He is just like a parent; we are not going to give our kids the things that they're not ready for. So the best thing we can do is get ourselves ready to receive.

How can we be good stewards of the gifts God wants to release to us? Once you align your identity with knowing who you are in Christ, it's like you've realize you're royalty! You're going to walk into a room and know that you're special and you come with authority. Just like a policeman enters a room everyone knows that his badge is a sign of his authority, you will say: "I know who I am in Christ. The enemy better move out of my way!" Instead of walking in timidly and backing down, you have the authority to arrest that meddling joker, because he has no rights over you. We need to ask ourselves what work we need to do in order to be responsible and ready.

Here's the thing: when you realize *who* you are and your true identity in Christ, you become dangerous to the enemy. When you realize that you have access to *dunamis* power (a Greek word describing the power that raised Jesus from the dead), spiritual authority, and God's favor to move mountains, you become unstoppable. The devil knows that when God's army is awake and fully armed we will destroy his evil works!

The enemy wants you to be weak; he wants you to cower in the corner with shame and blame. He wants you to be a victim so he can terrorize you. When you realize you have fire in you, you realize that you're fierce and fabulous because God made you that way! You start accepting your identity as it aligns with Jesus. Now because of anything you did or didn't do, but because of Jesus. That is why salvation is called a gift: you don't earn it, it's yours to have for free!

When you get your fierceness on you're going to walk in authority and power. You're going to wear your royal robe, and you're going to wear your crown. When you walk into a place, you're going to walk it like you own it, because you do! You can take ownership and control of the atmosphere in a place, because when you show up, the devil and his minions have to shut up and run. You start wielding your sword, and you get so much more effective that the enemy starts running when he sees you coming. You become more proactive and less defensive because you step out in authority and exercise your badge of authority!

Be Your Own Superhero

I love superhero movies. My favorite is *Wonder Woman*, obviously because her outfit is so fab and she knows how to kick butt! Another favorite movie of mine is *Captain Marvel*. Both these movies are a great way of visualizing what you look like in the spiritual realm.

If you think of yourself operating in the spiritual realm with the armor and tools of Wonder Women and the power of Captain Marvel, then you understand what it means to walk in your God-given authority. If you see yourself in the spirit like Wonder Woman, she has her armor, her weapons, and her shield. The armor of God is super important. This is tip number one: don't get out of your bed every morning until you're dressed completely in the armor of God.

We are constantly warring against the enemy. To be effective soldiers for God, we have to endure thorough training and refinement to learn how to wield our weapons. Sometimes the training is uncomfortable, and it's only when we humble ourselves that we are able to learn what there is to know. We have to be teachable and open to learning new methods so we can unlock the power of our weapons.

In the second Wonder Woman movie we get a glimpse of her as a child. We see her being trained by her aunt, alongside other adult warriors. The poignant scene is when she tries to cheat the system by getting ahead of other other competitors by sliding down an embankment. Just before she reaches the finishing line, her aunt rips her backwards, she falls over, and she loses the race (and is overtaken by everyone else). What we know as viewers is that she was not ready to take on the fight. Even though she knew she was destined for big things, the timing wasn't right, because she was not yet properly trained.

We have the same struggles with our walk with God. He gives us time to allow us to get ready for the battles ahead, He extends grace through timing. God is a gentleman. He is going to wait for our invitation. He will not force himself, or the mission, on us, until we are ready and willing to take instructions. That is why our biggest job is to be open. Be open and willing to say, "God, what is it that you want me to do? Help me partner with you and tell me what needs to be done." This is true surrender and obedience. No army can work at capacity if there are rogue soldiers going off in their own direction. We have to work as a cohesive unit and as a trusting team who will willingly take orders from our leader, God.

My favorite scene from the movie *Captain Marvel* is the one toward the end when she breaks free from her shackles. We see her on her knees in a solemn prayer position, constrained by electric-looking ties. In her mind's eye she is battling with the apparition of her old mentor, who we now know has been leading her astray. Just like the lies we deal with in our own minds, this mentor has been feeding her lies about her identity and her mission. The brilliant part is when she says, "I've been fighting with one arm behind my back. What happens when I'm finally set free?" Then she rips the sticker thingy off the back of her neck and explodes in power. She steps into her power and authority, and nothing can stop her!

My friend, you are Carol Danvers, also known as Captain Marvel. You have been fighting with one hand behind your back this whole time. You've been limited and unaware of your true potential and power. What if you too ripped off the shackles that bind you and finally let yourself free? You could have mighty weapons of warfare, but if you don't know how to use them, you're going to do some damage. So are you willing to go back to the drawing board? If so, get yourself ready to join the boot camp. Get ready to rid yourself of the junk in your trunk that is weighing you down. God needs you to be trained and strong so you know how to wield those weapons. Get ready to kick some butt!

Self-Reflection Exercise

Think about what motivates you:

- WHY do you do what you do?

- What motivates you to get out of bed in the morning?
- Decide what you want, e.g. increased confidence, financial freedom, peace of mind, healthy body, better opportunities, loving relationships, change lives, leave a legacy etc.
- Be SPECIFIC and write it down.

9

Power of Words

"You will continue to suffer if you have an emotional reaction to everything that is said to you. True power is observing things with logic. True power is restraint. If words control you, that means everyone else can control you. Breathe and allow things to pass."
Warren Buffet

A groundbreaking experiment conducted by Dr. Masura Emoto[22], a Japanese scientist, revolutionized the idea that our thoughts and intentions impact the physical realm. He studied the scientific evidence of how the molecular structure in water transforms when exposed to human words, thoughts, sounds, and intentions. He discovered that water is affected by a vibrational sound, using water sitting in a petri dish. The research included verbal affirmations, thoughts, music, and a prayer from a priest. He focused on verbal affirmations of love and gratitude.

He analyzed the water under a microscope. He took before and after pictures using what we call "magnetic resonance analysis technology" or high-speed photographs. He noticed beautiful crystals had formed in some of the frozen samples, where the positive vibrational waves were directed. What is amazing is that "love" and "gratitude" created crystals that look like a beautiful snowflake, while the words, "You disgust me," created an unrecognizable form. Words like "eternal," "peace," and "thank you" all formed beautiful structures, just like you would see in snowflakes and frozen water. Yet the concept of evil looked distorted and messy.

Dr. Emoto demonstrated how water exposed to loving, benevolent, and compassionate human intention results in aesthetically pleasing physical molecular formations in the water. While water exposed to fearful and discordant human intentions results in disconnected, disfigured, and unpleasant physical molecular formations.

This is amazing when you think about it. We think our words are just things we say, but when they go into the atmosphere, they actually have an effect.

With regards to music, Dr. Emoto demonstrated how certain types of sound—for instance, classical music like Mozart's Symphony Number 40—generated beautiful crystalline patterns, while others—like heavy metal music—generated ugly and distorted crystalline formations. In the images, you see the formations resulting from the two different types of music, and how really the big difference is knowing even what we listen to in music can directly affect our makeup in our bodies and brains. His research concluded that the power of sound is a vibration, and vibrations such as music and other positive words, including the human voice, can be a form of healing energy. He also illustrated that thoughts emit vibrations at frequencies we can't yet precisely determine, and they, too, have powers to harm or heal.

Sounds are waves or vibrations that ripple through the air unseen and provide humans with one of the most effective and vital ways to communicate with the nervous system. If you think about how your nervous system controls the body, from the information it receives, essentially telling the body how to react. For example, when you hear a car alarm, you immediately get frightened, and you think, "I must do something." Even an ice cream truck with elicits in children—and many adults!— the idea of fun and deliciousness. We know that the power of sound has a tremendous impact on us. Even if we don't actually see it, it is scientifically proven to affect us.

So consider the facts. If we look at nature, examine how vibrations travel via water in the air. If you throw a pebble into the water, you'll see ripples, and that effect creates sound. It's important to consider that our human bodies are made up of approximately 65 percent water, so it just makes you think, "What kinds of vibrations or sounds are we communicating to one another? What kind of energy are we producing for ourselves in the words that we speak over ourselves and for the rest of humanity through the words we speak about others?"

> *"The tongue has the power of life and death, and those who love it will eat its fruit."*
> *Proverbs 18:21, NIV*

Wielding Words for Good

This is profound when you think about how the Bible already confirmed this with Proverbs 18:21, the familiar, "Death and life are in the power of the tongue, and those who love it will eat its fruit." The Message translation is, "Words kill, words give life. They're either poison or fruit. You choose."

What words am I speaking? Consider these questions. How do you speak to yourself? How do you speak about others? How can you make better word choices? When do you censor your speech? What positive words can you start speaking? We need to consider this because sometimes we're so flippant about what we are saying, because of habits or perhaps how we were raised. We don't consider the effects of what we are saying.

It's also how you say things, your tone, that has a tremendous effect. Remember: what you focus on grows. If you are speaking words of hope and faith, oneness, forgiveness, kindness, and gratitude, then that is what you will get back. If you stand in a cave, and you shout out loud, the echo is going to reverb and come back at you. It's going to repeat what you have spoken. Consider this as your wake-up call to understanding and appreciating the words that we speak, both intentionally and unintentionally, and how we can fix it.

How to Recognize Words that Wound

Proverbs 16:24 (MSG) says, "Gracious speech is like clover honey; good taste for the soul, quick energy for the body."

Withering Words

Our mouth gets us in a whole lot of trouble. We can determine the success of our day simply by how we speak. What is the first thing that you say in the morning? "I'm feeling good. I'm feeling great." Or perhaps it's something else. We can immediately tell the health of a person's soul by the standard of their speech, because a wounded soul speaks out of the mouth. It's critical that we censor our speech, becoming aware of what we're saying, and how we are saying it. Because just like Jesus, who caused the tree to wither by simply cursing it with these words, our own withering words can cause the fruits of our gifts, talents, relationships, and future to wither. We can live the results of either our withered or our fruitful words.

Flippant Words

As a modern society, we use colloquial words as part of our speech, and we've become so blinded by their power. We've become so flippant with our speech that we have become numb to the negative effects. Perhaps you've been pronouncing word curses over yourself and you didn't even know it. We can use our words to judge and condemn people without knowing it. We may use teasing or sarcastic words that we think are funny, but are actually wounding to others. Think about the importance of a marriage vow. Why do people say, "I will be your wife," or, "I will be your husband?" It's because it's a sacred event. When two souls agree with their mouths to be married and tied for life, God takes these vows very seriously.

Damaging Words

Things like lies and omissions of truth also fall within a category of negative words. We cannot take back words once the damage is done. But we can use our words by agreeing with God's Word to bring health in healing. We have the power to loose or bind on earth what is in heaven. Sometimes it's not what we say, but also what we do not say that keeps us stuck. If we keep professing negative words over ourselves, but we never add the positive words back, we keep ourselves stuck. Perhaps you've said things like, "I'm not good enough. Nobody likes me. I'm stupid. I always get it wrong. I'm accident prone. You're killing me. It's to die for. I feel dead. You're driving me crazy. I'm sick and tired and I'm losing my sanity." A lot of these flippant words are spoken in our society, but words are containers of power. We need to know the importance of what we're saying and how we're saying it.

Words are containers of power.

Complaining

Complaining and grumbling are negative. Our mouths get us into so much trouble. When we complain, we shut down the heavens over us. We could be praying for answers, and God has sent the answer in a package ready to be delivered to our address. But every time you complain, it hits the pause button on the conveyor belt of progress, and the package gets delayed. Often the package gets delivered, but you're so busy fretting on Worry Way, grumbling on Lament Lane, or complaining on Complaint's Corner that you're not home to receive it and miss your blessing, or the package might even get sent back to sender. How can we frame this to create steps to success? The first thing is to reflect on your words. Awareness is key. How has your speech impacted your mindset, your emotions, and your circumstances? Write down the words you feel are not serving you. Decide what needs to go. Make a list of words to then replace the negative words. For example, instead of saying, "I'm broken," replace that with, "I'm a work in progress." Make it your intention to censor your speech by becoming aware of the words that are harming you.

How to Reform your Words

Andrew Newberg, MD, and Mark Robertson Waldman wrote the book [23]*How God Changes Your Brain: Breakthrough Findings from a Leading Neuroscientist.* They say that a single word has the power to influence the expression of genes that regulate physical and emotional stress. This is a truth bomb. Sticks and stones may break your bones, but words can change your brain. The power of words is significant.

According to Newberg and Waldman, words can literally change your brain:

> A single word has the power to influence the expression of genes that regulate physical and emotional stress. Positive words, such as "peace" and "love," can alter the expression of genes, strengthening areas in our frontal lobes and promoting the brain's cognitive functioning. They propel the motivational centers of the brain into action, and build resiliency.

Newberg and Waldman go on to write:

> Conversely, hostile negative language can disrupt specific genes that play a key part in the production of neurochemicals that protect us from stress. Humans are hardwired to worry. Part of our primal brain is built to protect us from threats to our survival. Angry words send alarm messages through the brain, and they partially shut down the logic-and reasoning centers located in the frontal lobes.

According to the authors, using the right words can transform your reality. You stimulate frontal lobe activity when you hold a positive and optimistic word in your mind. This area includes specific language centers that connect directly to the motor cortex that is responsible for moving you into action. As their research has shown, the longer you concentrate on positive words, the more you begin to affect other areas of the brain.

Positive words like "peace" and "love" can alter the expression of your genes, strengthen areas in your frontal lobe, and promote the brain's cognitive functioning. They propel the motivational centers of the brain into action and build resiliency. Humans are hardwired to worry. Our brains are programmed to avoid discomfort. So any choice we make is really your brain's first reaction to the question, "Is this going to be uncomfortable? Is this going to make me happy?" Because part of our primal brain makeup is to protect us from threats to our survival.

Naturally, our thoughts are the first to react to any given threat. We've all heard of the fight or flight or fear response. A single negative word can increase the activity in your amygdala, which is the fear center of the brain. This releases dozens of stress producing hormones and neurotransmitters, which interrupts your brain's functioning like logic, reason, and language. Speaking angry words sends alarm messages through the brain, and they partially shut down the logic and reasoning centers located in the frontal lobes. This is exactly why when you are being yelled at, you probably don't remember what the argument was about or what was being said. Your brain tries to protect you from the threat or trauma and shuts down any reasoning, which often happens with abuse. Verbal abuse creates this response that you can't actually remember and it physiologically affects how your brain functions. Instead, the longer you concentrate on positive words, the more you begin to affect other areas of your brain. By holding a positive and optimistic word in your mind, you can stimulate your frontal lobe activity. And this has all been done through brain scans; they've actually proven this through science. This affects the language centers responsible for moving you into action.

You heard of the whole freeze mode, right? This is when someone yells at you or something negative happens and you just can't think and you can't move. In these cases, using positive words changes your perception of yourself and the people you interact with. A positive view of yourself will bias you towards seeing the good in others, whereas a negative self-image will cause suspicion and doubt. If you start criticizing others and seeing the flaws in others, and seeing the flaws in yourself, it can be like a house of cards: it just comes tumbling down.

Over time, the structure of your thalamus will also change in response to your conscious words, thoughts, and feelings. These thalamic changes in your brain affect the way you perceive reality. So if you are constantly exposing and seeing the negative in others, criticizing others, being judgmental, and speaking negative words over other people, you start to wire your brain to look for more negativity.

If you think about TV programs like *Survivor* ("You're voted off the island"), or talent competitions, you're looking to dismiss or exclude them. It's actually a negative way of approaching things, because your brain starts to look for the same repeatable patterns. If you are repeating a negative pattern, it's going to keep finding the same thing. Truth bomb. Your conscious thoughts, words, and feelings will actually change your reality and how you view life.

Here are some positive words you can use to start to replace the negative words: abundant, accomplished, beloved, blessed, challenged, confident, daring, disciplined, empowered, extraordinary, exuberant, fabulous, fantastic, forgiven, free, glorious, gutsy, happy, honored, inspired, innovative, joyful, magnificent, marvelous, majestic, opportunity, overjoyed, passionate, popular, powerful, prosperous, protected, purposeful, qualified, radiant, relevant, revolutionary, remarkable, rich, resilient, satisfied, significant, smart, successful, talented, tenacious, terrific, transformed, trustworthy, triumphant, unlimited, unstoppable, valuable, victorious, worthy.

Now think for a minute. The challenge in the test. What positive words made you feel uncomfortable? Why do you think they made you feel uncomfortable? What words challenged you? What words inspired you? What words do you aim to achieve and embody? What words are you going to start using so you can move towards believing what you say about yourself?

"A man sees in the world what he carries in his heart."
Johann Wolfgang von Goethe

The sooner we become aware of our words and how we speak about ourselves and others, the sooner we can directly change how we perceive our world. If you can be more aware of your words, it might inspire you to speak the words more intentionally before you feel their negative effects. Your motivation and your feelings will follow. But first you need to start to speak the words with a positive mindset.

Here are some positive statements you can use to wield your words for good:

- I believe my circumstances do not define my ability to succeed.
- I believe that my intelligence, talents and gifts are not what creates success.
- I believe that my identity is not found in what I do but in who I am.
- I believe there are no failures only experiments that help me get closer to my success.
- I believe that learning is my priority to keep stretching myself beyond where I currently am.
- I believe that I am the boss of my brain!

Self-Reflection Exercise

Let's use ACT (Acceptance and Commitment Therapy) and imagine an important moment where you would be celebrating you in some way. Think of an important life transition or moment.

- Where would this moment be?
- What would your friends and family be saying about you?
- What would be the most meaningful thing that someone might say to you in this moment or this setting?

What comes up for you is going to reveal a meaningful value area of your life. What people say about you is going to reveal a personal quality you appreciate about yourself.

10

Habit Reinvention

"The formula for success is surprisingly simple. It's just a few acts of self-discipline practiced daily over a reasonable period of time."
Jim Rohn

Do you ever feel you're stuck in a rut? That you can't seem to break free of the bad habits that are keeping you from reaching your goals? You're not alone. Billions of people around the world struggle with habit formation every day. What if I told you it didn't have to be this way? What if there was a science to habit formation, and once you understood it, creating good habits became easy?

How to Form a New Habit (Or Break an Old One)

We all have habits. Whether or not we realize it, habits are a big part of our lives. They dictate how we behave on a day-to-day basis. And while some habits are good (like brushing our teeth), others can be bad (like biting our nails).

How do you form a new habit and break an old one? It seems like everyone has their own method, and it's hard to know what works and what doesn't. We are going to discuss the science of habits—how they work, why they're so important, and how to go about forming or breaking them.

Habits are behaviors we do unconsciously daily. They can be good habits, like brushing our teeth before bed, or bad habits, like eating unhealthy foods. Habits are hard to break but even harder to form. It takes time, effort, and consistency to create a new habit and even more time and effort to get rid of an old one.

If you're like most people, you probably want to be healthier, more productive, and happier. But it's not always easy to change our behavior. That's because forming good habits is hard! It takes time and effort to create new patterns of behavior that become automatic.

What Are Habits and How Are They Formed?

A habit is simply a pattern of behavior that is repeated regularly and often automatically. We form habits through a process called "chunking." This is when the brain takes a series of individual actions and links them together to make a new behavior. For example, if you always brush your teeth after you wake up, your brain has chunked those two behaviors together.

There are four main stages to habit formation:

- The cue: This is the trigger that tells your brain it's time to start a particular behavior. For example, the cue for brushing your teeth might wake you up in the morning.
- The routine: This is the actual behavior that you perform. In our example, the routine of brushing your teeth.
- The reward: This reinforces the behavior so that your brain wants to do it again in the future. The reward for brushing your teeth might be the feeling of cleanliness or the taste of minty toothpaste.
- The craving: This drives us to repeat the behavior even when we don't want to. We often relate cravings to the reward we receive from the behavior. For example, we might brush our teeth even when we're tired because we crave the feeling of cleanliness that comes with it.

"We first make our habits, and then our habits make us."
John Dryden

How Habits Are Reformed

If you have had habits for a few years it's safe to say it's going to take a little while to rewire those habits. Dr. Caroline Leaf[24] talks about how it takes a minimum of sixty-three days to change an automated habit, not just twenty-one days as we previously thought. This is why I like a ninety-day plan: because it is achievable. We are not daunting our brain to think of a long time period; instead we are giving it the opportunity for small wins.

Following a process for the first ninety days helps you to push past the initial fear. Once we have momentum, we need to persist through the "messy middle." It's the stage where you've broken the car down into parts, so there is not going back. But you can't see the final product yet, and it feels frustrating. It feels like nothing is growing or changing. Whether you are writing a book, renovating your house, or doing an exercise routine, the messy middle is always hard. This is when a lot of people give up, because they're not seeing the results they want to see.

The trick is to keep going until it becomes a new muscle memory. Keep up your momentum until you stop thinking about it and your brain stops resisting you. Eventually, it will feel safe and achievable. You've just got to hold your ground while your toddler and teenage brain have a meltdown!

The next stage is following the process for another ninety days to really reinforce it. I would say if you really want to do anything, realistically you need to invest six months. If you are willing, you will be prepared and persistent. You will be willing to put up with the challenges because you know that there is no instant quick fix. You are in it for the long haul.

Here is the good news: once you've developed a new habit and you've made the new habit a muscle memory, in the future it's going to be so much easier. It's not going to take nearly as much energy, and you're going to be so much more efficient. It's like getting in a vehicle with premium grade fuel. You're going to get there so much more smoothly at the highest speed. It will be more enjoyable and you will drive in style. Personally, I think that's a much better way to travel.

Small Changes, Big Results

There's a principle called "Kaizen,"[25] which refers to a Japanese word that means "improvement or change." Kaizen has five principles translated to English, which are "sought, organized, declutter, standardization, and self-discipline."

We often convince ourselves that massive success requires massive action and that we only can be successful if we take huge leaps. However, small habits make a big difference. Small improvements, even 1 percent, aren't notable at first, but compounds in the future. Improving by 1 percent each day for one year, and you'll end up 365 times better by the end of the year. On the flip side, if you get 1 percent worse every day for a year, you will decline to nearly zero by the end of the year. This is why it's so important to understand that small wins or minor setbacks accumulate over time.

The facts are that habits are a result of compound interest in self-improvement. The slow pace of transformation can make it easy to let a bad habit slide. Outcomes are a delayed measure of your habits repeated over time. Just like a rudder of a ship, slight changes in your daily habits can guide your life to a very different destination. Just think: one degree on an ocean liner can change its trajectory and its destination over time. The key simply is just to stay the course.

"Discipline is the bridge between goals and accomplishments."
Jim Rohn

Jim Rohn says, "Discipline is the bridge between goals and accomplishments." I love this picture because it is so true to life, sports, and business. Often we look at people and we think, "Wow, look at them. They did so great. They won and they got their awards," and we cheer for them. But what we don't see is what is called the "iceberg effect." It's the things that compounded underneath, in order to build to where they are now. For someone to win a race, we can't discount the desire, passion, focus, failure, training, effort, pain, injury, hard work, late nights, early morning, sacrifice, listening, fear, time, and support.

The list goes on and on. But we make the mistake of thinking people have overnight success, because we haven't seen the work that they've done to build the blocks towards their success. We can't always assume that what we see is easy. If people do say it's easy, then they're lying—because it definitely is not!

The truth about progress is that breakthroughs are often the result of several previous actions that build up the potential needed to unleash major change—just like dynamite compounded together can make a huge explosion. Habits often appear to make no difference until you cross the threshold and unlock a new level of performance.

Many people—whether it's running their business, writing a book, losing weight, or running a race—don't have the patience to get through what we call the messy middle or the valley of disappointment. Because this is where most people give up, give in, and walk away thinking they're just not making any progress. They're not seeing the weight drop off them, they're not seeing the growth they saw in the beginning, they're not seeing the money accumulate in their bank account quickly enough.

The hallmark of any compounding process is that the most powerful outcomes are delayed. Put simply: don't give up. Just like putting money in the bank, if you put a few cents in over a few years, it's going to compound with interest and then you'll be able to see the benefits. What you focus on grows and time magnifies the margin between success and failure. It multiplies whatever you feed it. So you put the effort in, and you get the effort out. It might not be an overnight success like winning the jackpot, because those wins are very far and few between. It simply is staying the course.

Slow and steady wins the race.

The Plateau and the Messy Middle

Let's consider what it means to persist beyond the plateau. If you think of when you are first learning something new, often you follow the hockey stick learning trajectory. It's where you get momentum really quickly and your learning curve is steep. But then you get to the plateau, where things seem to level out. Beginner's luck seems to fade and then it becomes hard work. What we need to remember is even though you're consistently putting in that effort, the effort is not wasted. It's just simply stored for another day. At the right time and at the right place, everything will compound. When it's time to cash in, then you will see the results.

Having a goal-oriented mindset creates this yo-yo effect. It's up and it's down, and it's up and it's down. You feel good, then you feel bad. Focusing on big goals causes you to put off any kind of fulfillment or happiness until the next milestone is achieved. It's saying, "I won't be happy until I lose fifty pounds." That is a huge milestone! How about you start with losing just two? This delayed progress can be demotivating, which is often why people give up. When you think about weight loss, people in the beginning might see the weight shed off quickly. But those in the messy middle don't see as much gain or progress. It can be demotivating when you don't see the results you want. Nothing has gone wrong if your progress has slowed; it is perfectly normal. The key is not to give up!

Goals versus Systems

Goals are good for setting a direction of where you want to go, but having systems is how you actually progress. When it gets to the messy middle, having a system that you're following through helps you keep swimming. Follow the system and just put one foot in front of the other. Knowing you are trusting the process and the system is really where the success lies. Focus more on the growth process than the ultimate outcome, so you can stay motivated to press on and move forward. In life, success always appears to be a straight line from the bottom to the top, right? What people think it looks like and what it really looks like is a little step forward and a few steps back. You may have to repeat and do it again, but the whole key is to simply keep moving.

Habits and Identity

"We first make our habits and then our habits make us."
John Dryden

John Dryden says, "We first make our habits and then our habits make us." Your identity and who you think you are emerges out of your habits. Every belief about yourself is learned through conditioning and your experiences. The whole concept of nature versus nurture is debatable: from your family culture, how you were raised, your beliefs, your convictions, your habits, and your mindsets. That is made up of who you become. So your personality is a makeup of who you are at birth, as well as what you were taught. But not everything that we were taught or learned serves us, so we need to choose to change. Becoming the best version of yourself is going to require you to adjust your beliefs, upgrade your identity, and expand your thinking. Decide on the person you want to be and prove it to yourself by celebrating small wins.

Identifying Harmful Habits

Ask yourself these questions: Do you repeatedly hear the same critique from others? Do you find yourself acting extra defensive over something you say or do? Do you resonate or get irritated with someone else's insecurity and you try to fix it in them? Have you noticed a pattern of people reacting negatively to something you say and do? Have you noticed a repeated pattern of behavior in your family and relationships? Is there a habit you have that perhaps irritates, upsets, or disturbs a loved one, family member, or colleague? Is there something that you keep doing that you know you shouldn't, but you continue to do it anyway?

Your body will show you warning signals, and it's important to consider your emotional and physical warning signals. They are a reason to pay attention, not to simply ignore and just to press on. Sometimes it's good to press on, but some of the time, just like if you put your hand on a hot stove, your body is going to make you want to retract your hand because it's painful.

In modern society, we placate or sugarcoat or distract ourselves with things to not deal with the signs. So consider this: what are you sensing from your subconscious mind that you've become aware of that upsets you and others? What are the habits that you are acting out when you feel anxious, worried, rushed, stressed, angry, emotional, triggered? What is the common denominator that messes up your relationships? And what are those triggers? Become aware of what they are, when your body reacts and your heart starts palpitating, when you start to feel like adrenaline is pumping through your veins. What were you thinking, and what were you doing in that moment that triggered that response? Start to think about what you are thinking about.

Toxic Habits

These are habits that you might have developed through conditioning, experience, nurturing, and environment. They result in certain behaviors that are not exactly good for you, and they create negative behavioral patterns that are repeated. Some of them can be considered people pleasing, being argumentative and defensive, perhaps being easily irritated, snapping at loved ones, a lack of patience, excessive worrying, ruminating or over analyzing, poor sleeping patterns, unhealthy eating and diet, a lack of exercise. All of these affect our mental and physical health. They also affect those around us, because if we're not feeling good, and we are in this habit of toxic thinking and toxic speech and toxic habits, it affects everybody around us. The problem is that we're not wired for toxicity. The destructive habits cause loads of toxic stress in our physical, mental, and emotional well being. Toxic stress has been proven to affect our mental, physical, and emotional states. Just think: if you get anxious about something, your body reacts with stomach aches and headaches and feeling sweaty. Toxic stress affects our hormones, adrenals, digestion, mental processing, sleeping, diet choices, and the list goes on and on. We can't simply just address the symptom like, "I have a headache, I'm going to pop a pill." We have to address the root cause. If we know what the cause is, what the root is, we can then address that so we don't have to repeat those patterns.

Steps to Success

It's important to reflect and stand back and look at yourself objectively, like you're watching a movie of your life. You need to separate your who, which is your identity and who you are at the core, from your do, which is your actions and habits. Perhaps you might have a habit of being angry and being short-tempered. It doesn't necessarily mean that you're a bad person. It just means you've developed a habit of coping that's not necessarily serving you. Remember: there is no room for shame, condemnation, or victimization.

Do you see the need to change? And why? Can you trace the origin of this toxic habit? When did it start? Write down your answers. No ideas are bad ideas. Then reflect and look back at what you've written. Look at it objectively. Then think about an alternate behavior that you can replace with the toxic habit. Prioritize your toxic habits and select the most dominant ones to work on first. Don't get overwhelmed if you have a long list of things that you know you want to work on. Let's tackle the most dominant one and then work your way through that and celebrate the wins.

A great tool to use is Dr. Caroline Leaf's version of mind mapping, which she calls a "metacog." It's where you write down something like, "Okay, this is the problem," and you start to branch off ideas of what you think could be solutions.

Perhaps if I get angry in traffic, maybe I need to leave a little earlier, or maybe I need to prepare the night before, or maybe I need to make sure that everybody knows the plan for the next day. What are those things that you know that you can do to preempt that behavior instead of just constantly reacting? This mind mapping technique works great in all forms when you're trying to figure out a problem. It helps you do a brain dump and take what's worrying you from your subconscious mind, and put it on paper to the forefront of your mind. This will help you to actually address it and is a great tool to use to further your mindsets, habits, and routines.

Set reminders on your phone or post a sticky note on your refrigerator every time that you find yourself doing this repeated behavior. You're going to remind yourself of what to do. So every time you feel toxic habits or thoughts and emotions, tell yourself, "It's okay to analyze that I'm doing something wrong, but only if I grasp the lesson. So, what is the lesson here?" If for example you get a traffic ticket, instead of getting angry you could say: "Okay, what's the lesson? I was going too fast. I wasn't paying attention to my surroundings. So, I need to know that that is a warning signal."

It's important to listen to your warning signals. Acknowledge them without getting in a panic. Think about them as a tool to help you readjust. Take a deep breath and decide on a calm action. What will you do and say that moves you away from this toxic habit? Continue this practice for a minimum of twenty-one days each time you encounter a challenging habit, emotion, or thought. Keep a record of your progress because that's how the progress is going to keep you motivated. Then continue exercising your new skill for sixty-three days until it becomes a lifestyle habit. Just like when you learned to drive. At first it seemed a little uncomfortable, you didn't know the rules of the road, and it felt a little scary when you're going at speed. But eventually you were cruising on the highway without even thinking about it. Now you can hold a conversation, listen to music, and drive at the same time because muscle memory has taken over.

This whole process is mind hacking our brains to start to think of a new journey, creating a new path of thinking and processing.

How to Form a Good Habit

Now that we understand how habits are formed, let's talk about how you can use this knowledge to your advantage. If you want to form a new habit, the best thing to do is to start small. Choose a cue and a routine that you can easily implement into your daily life. For example, if you want to work out, your cue could be to put on your workout clothes as soon as you wake up. And your routine could be to do a quick, ten-minute workout. As you form the habit, you can increase the length and intensity of your workouts.

It's also important to make sure that your new habit has a clear reward associated with it. This will help your brain to want to repeat the behavior in the future. For our example, the reward could be the feeling of accomplishment after completing a workout or the endorphins that are released during exercise.

Finally, it's essential to have a plan for when cravings strike. Cravings are normal and they're going to happen, especially in the beginning. But if you have a plan for how you're going to deal with them, they'll be much easier to overcome. For example, if you're trying to cut back on drinking soda, your plan might be to drink a glass of water instead whenever you have a craving.

Habit formation is a complex process, but if you understand the science behind it, you can use that knowledge to your advantage. So what are you waiting for? Start small and begin forming the habits that will help you reach your goals!

Self-Reflection Exercise

- Assess your behavior and decide which habits are helping you grow, and which are limiting you.
- Write down recurring challenges you encounter, like repeating patterns of behavior.

II

Unlock Your Mind

11

Pivot, Adapt, Opportunity

"If you change the way you look at things, the things you look at change."
Wayne Dyer

My friends and clients laugh at me when I tell them to, "Get your head out of the chicken coop!" I love this analogy, because when we can compare the differences between chickens and eagles, we can relate it to our own behavior.

Chickens versus Eagles

Chicken Facts

Chickens spend approximately 61 percent of their time foraging, pecking, and scratching for food[26]. The chicken pecking order is a natural part of chicken behavior. When exposed to stress due to limited access to food, water, sunlight, and space, they become overly aggressive and attack each other. When you reduce the need to compete for basic needs, chickens settle down and are kinder to each other[27]. If you've observed feeding time at a farm, you will notice that chickens mimic behavior. They can get each other in a tizzy when a limited amount of feed is thrown into a coop; mayhem breaks out!

99

Eagle Facts

Bald Eagles tend to soar alone, rather than flocking with other eagles[28]. They select a breeding territory after evaluating if it will supply their needs for food, nesting, and isolation from excessive human activity. Eagles are monogamous; they mate for life and use the same nest each year[29]. The bald eagle is an excellent predator that has adapted to different habitats and lifestyles. Their extraordinary vision allows them to spot prey from far away distances. Their large wingspan enables them to soar high above their targets, before swooping down for an attack. Their powerful talons allow them to snatch their meals from the water's surface or pluck their prey from the ground or air. Bald eagles tend to hunt in pairs which gives them an advantage over solo predators, because they use their combined strength and strategy to take down larger animals with ease[30].

As humans we exhibit the same behavior as chickens when feeling stressed. We act aggressively toward one another out of scarcity and fear. We tend to focus on our immediate problems, like our next paycheck, with little consideration for the future. We fight over the limited "seed" that gets thrown into the coop, thinking we won't have enough for tomorrow. We live under lack and limits with little room for leisurely thinking. Our perspective is limited, and we can't imagine another life could exist outside the chicken coop.

"But those who hope in the Lord will renew their strength. They will soar on wings like eagles; they will run and not grow weary, they will walk and not be faint."
Isaiah 40:31, NIV

An eagle rises above the noise of the frey, and does not take the bait to get sucked into pecking and clucking like the chickens. Eagles love the storm and welcome the challenges it brings. Eagles use air currents to lift themselves to new heights and to gain perspective of how small the world (and their problems) are below. Eagles have excellent vision and concentration and can focus on one thing at a time. An eagle is not rushed to act and takes its time to see far into the distance to weigh up its options. Eagles prefer to fly alone, away from the noise and distractions. They hunt in pairs because they know their combined strengths dramatically improves their chances of success. The eagle is a master of change management and rises above its challenges and pain. What if we could zoom out like the eagle to a ten-thousand-foot viewpoint, and switch our thinking?

Change Is Good

Our world is in transition. We can't deny that things are changing. Change can be good when we change our outlook, our perspective, and our viewpoint. We don't have to accept everything at face value, especially the negative things you hear on the news. Asking questions makes you smarter. Asking God what His plans are for your life will open up a brand new world of opportunities for you. Let's discuss how we can pivot, adapt and look for opportunities amidst the storm.

Uniqueness

It has always fascinated me to look at the uniqueness of personality types in the world. You get the entrepreneurial types and those who are sticklers for rules and who need conformity. Apparently, more structured personalities are less than 3 percent of the population. This means 97 percent of our population are more experiential in their learning. It's strange to me that our school systems have primarily catered to the 3 percent.

This leaves us with the systemic problem we have today. The majority of the population will ask "Why?" before they will color inside the lines. It's tough as a parent to gauge this well, but I have raised my three children to think for themselves and to ask questions. They need to be equipped in such a way that they are able to step back and look at things from an eagle-eyed view.

We don't have to accept everything at face value, because asking
"Why?" makes you smarter.

Questioning the status quo gives you the chance to learn, to look a little deeper, and to figure out the reasons behind things. In South Africa, culturally, we are taught not to rely on the government for healthcare or retirement. Crime is so prevalent in the country and so many live below the poverty line. It's up to the individual to look out for their own retirement and healthcare plans.

I think because I was raised in an unstable environment, I have learned how to take care of myself and to figure things out without the support of others.

Those who know me know about my rants about the educational system. In my view, we are teaching our kids to memorize facts, but we're not teaching them to think. Everything we decide on today will have a repercussion in the next five or ten or even fifty years. Perhaps it's time for us to teach our children that the decisions they make today are strategic for their future.

Is college or university right for every personality? Maybe we need to consider that what suits one doesn't suit all. Before they get stuck in a system that might not be what they're designed for, why don't we teach them to ask the right questions first?

The lie we have believed is that the only way to be successful in today's world is to get a college degree. However, many entrepreneurs don't see the value of a college degree and yet are doing exceptionally well.

I had a conversation about "adulting" with one of my young adult children. I explained that this is when the rules of the game change. This is when you must take ownership and responsibility for your own life. It can be tough, and things don't always go according to plan, but you have to embrace the mindset of growth and learning even when things suck.

As a parent, put them in the environment and let them grow.

As parents, we have to be okay with allowing our kids to fail and to learn from their choices and mistakes. If our kids don't "make the grade" or make poor decisions, the only way they will grow their own mind muscles is if we don't always step in to rescue them.

We do this because of our own set of expectations we place on ourselves about our parenting. We worry about what the girl next door is doing with her life, and we feel the pressure to measure up. These expectations are simply not helpful for everyone involved.

I like to see the positive side of life's challenges. For example, we all lived through the pandemic but it hasn't been all bad. We've learned different ways of adapting. Before teachers were used to being in a classroom; now they have had to learn how to teach kids online. With online schooling, you don't have an automatic feedback loop like you do in a classroom. The teacher has to allow students time to absorb and process information. We all have had to adapt the ways we teach, learn, and think.

Back in the old days, farmers needed kids to help them out with harvesting crops during the summer months. In the United States, kids would start their school year after the harvest, usually after the Labor Day holiday. This means that kids are given a three-month vacation! Today we don't need our kids working on farms anymore; we need them learning in classrooms! The world needs all kinds of unique personalities, so our educational system should not be one size fits all.

If we truly connected people to their purpose and their unique strengths, can you imagine how amazing the world would be? Artisans, musicians, entrepreneurs, writers, singers, and mathematicians all singing to their own unique tune. What a magical and beautiful symphony it would be!

Teaching an Old Dog New Tricks

True story: I became a competitive adult figure skater at the age of thirty-one. I had never learned to ice skate when I was a child, but I was a classically trained ballet dancer. This meant that I had to learn from scratch. People said I was crazy. However, I believe in the possibilities of growth, and I saw how possible it is to reprogram the brain through neuroscience. It's a challenge. I fall, I learn, and I grow through the training. Having a positive mindset towards doing something new is the key to overcoming the fear. The good news is that I'm proof that you can teach an old dog new tricks!

Elon Musk and I attended the same high school in South Africa, and I was a few years behind him. Considering the rigid environment we were raised in, and its intolerance for anything outside the box, I know exactly what he went through (having been bullied myself). Back then, daydreaming of becoming a rocket scientist was a far stretch for a South African school kid—yet look at him today!

We have to be willing to dream big. Then we will be able to teach our children to dream big too, work hard, and learn despite their challenges. We will fall down, we will fail, but that's okay. Because every time you fail, you learn how to get up again.

> *"If you don't like something, change it. If you can't change it, change your attitude."*
> *Maya Angelou*

Change is a natural and necessary part of life, but it's difficult to let go of the old and comfortable. Change is an inevitable part of life, and if you're not ready for it, you might find yourself behind. Are you embracing change in your life?

Change Is Good: How to Embrace Change in Your Life

Many people resist change, fearing that it will bring instability and chaos into their lives. Not to mention that change can be scary! However, embracing change can actually lead to growth and happiness. If you're willing to break out of your comfort zone and embrace a growth mindset, anything is possible.

Tips to Embrace Change and Grow from It

1. Let go of the past

One of the best things you can do when embracing change is to let go of the past. This includes any negative thoughts or memories that are holding you back. It's important to focus on the present and future, and not dwell on what has already happened.

2. Be ready to move on

When you're embracing change, it's important to be ready to move on from the past. This means being willing to leave behind old habits and ways of thinking. It's difficult to do this because the brain prefers comfort, but it's necessary in order to make room for fresh growth.

3. Break through obstacles

Accept the fact that there will be obstacles in your way when you're embracing change. It's important to identify these obstacles and overcome them. This may mean seeking help from others or taking some time for yourself to reflect and grow.

4. Change is like grieving

Letting go of the old way of doing things and embracing the new can be difficult, and it's often compared to grieving. It's important to allow yourself to experience all the stages of grief: denial, anger, bargaining, depression, then acceptance.

5. Breach your comfort zone

In order to grow, you need to be open to press through to breach your comfort zone. This means being willing to try new things and take risks outside of your comfort zone. It can be scary and uncomfortable, but it's essential for personal growth.

6. Embrace a growth mindset

One of the best things you can do when embracing change is to adopt a growth mindset. This means believing that you can grow and improve. It's an incredibly powerful way of thinking that will help you succeed in all areas of life.

7. Overcome your fear of change and embrace the unknown

Embracing change can be difficult, but it's necessary in order to grow and improve. Embrace change in your life so that you can reap the many benefits that come with it.

Self-Reflection Exercise

- What do you need to let go of?
- Identify the obstacles holding you back.
- What can you do today that will stretch you past your comfort zone?

12

Challenging Limiting Beliefs

"The mind is just like a muscle—the more you exercise it, the stronger it gets and the more it can expand."
Idowu Koyenikan

Do you secretly desire to become more successful without sacrificing peace, relationships, and happiness? Perhaps you're on a journey to make a big impact and to leave a legacy. Maybe you feel called, and know you're destined for greatness, but you need a little help putting things together?

Here's a question: Have you ever felt stuck with a lack of progress, as if you're swimming upstream against the current? I'm sure there have been many opportunities in life where you've been challenged with this. Perhaps you have felt that no matter how hard you try, it feels like its taking two steps forward, then one step back. Maybe you make a little bit of progress, and then life happens, so it feels like you are constantly swimming against the current.

The river is a metaphor for life. The river of life is always flowing, and we don't see what is up ahead of us or downstream, only the water in front of us. We don't know where it started or how it began, but the river of life is always flowing.

Sometimes we may find ourselves in the river of misery, battling to keep our heads above water. In a panic, our tendency is to flap about, thrash, and fight the current. We have a survival instinct to exert lots of effort to fight where we are. But we end up going against the current and using way more energy than we need to.

We need to embrace where the current is taking us, so we can go with the flow of the river and find refreshment in it. Instead of fighting it, wishing it would return to where it once was, we need to embrace the season of cleansing and refreshment, especially when the Lord is leading us to discover new waters. We want to open our mind, our heart, and our life to what needs to be changed so that we are not fighting ourselves and the current. We can use the flow of the river to get us where we want to go much more quickly.

Built Like a Salmon

Let me tell you what I've learned about salmon as it relates to this concept. They are designed to swim upstream. When it's time for them to mate and to start the next cycle of life, they know exactly what they need to do to get back upstream. Salmon have the fortitude and the mission-minded focus that no matter how hard the current is, they know they are built to make it up the river.

Become like a salmon and go with the flow when you need to, but know you have what it takes within you to swim upstream when it's needed. You may have forgotten your identity, but the good news is that it's not your fault. Sometimes it's going to feel like you can't get where you want to be, because your brain is putting the brakes on your potential.

Your brain is putting the brakes on your potential.

Stars in the Sky

Your brain's main function is to keep you safe. It's wired to avoid discomfort. The brain uses 20 percent of your oxygen and blood flow. Did you know that there are more connections in your brain than there are stars in the sky?

Our primitive brain is wired to avoid discomfort, which is what I call the "two-year-old toddler having a tantrum." It doesn't like it if it doesn't have its way. The good news is you can retrain your brain through choice. Through practice and intentional choice, you can discipline that toddler in your brain.

The other good news is that you are not stuck with the brain you have. You can't actually age backwards, according to Dr. Daniel Amen[31]. You can change your brain to change your life.

When faced with a choice, your brain refers to old patterns, habits, and experiences to determine if this choice is safe or not. If you've had a good experience, it will think, "Okay, this is safe. Let's proceed." If you've been disappointed by something or someone, it's a little harder to convince your brain to push through. For example, if you've tried a restaurant, and you didn't like the food the first time, usually what happens is you don't want to repeat that experience and never return. It's just your brain's way of keeping you safe.

However, can you really trust your brain? Can you rely on your brain's programming to make the best choice for you every time? Just think about it for a minute. As a child, maybe you made a choice for safety reasons, and perhaps your brain is still thinking that that programming needs to serve you now. But as an adult, you've learned a few things and realized, "I don't know if that's serving me any more." Unfortunately, our brain is still stuck in that gear of thinking that this is how you make this decision. It's kind of like when you're driving a car in stick shift; you need to get it out of that gear and into the next gear, which will take you where you want to go.

Why You Are Stuck

Perhaps the reason why you are stuck is because your childhood memories and experiences that have been stored in your brain as "truth" are blocking you. But ask yourself: Is it the truth? Maybe it's not the complete truth, or the complete picture. Have you ever challenged those thoughts or questioned why you believe what you believe?

Circumstances are a result of choices, and choices are a result of the thoughts and beliefs we have. If someone has strong beliefs and values, it's very difficult to change that person's course or path. The same thing happens with negative beliefs. Weighing up too many options can result in inactivity and staying stuck. Your heart is yearning for one thing, but your head is saying another thing. That in-between tug of war feels very frustrating. It's like having a car that's stuck in the mud. You might put more pressure on the pedal thinking that the harder you push, the faster you'll go. But all you're doing is spinning mud, because you're staying stuck in inactivity. You can't go anywhere, and that's why you're stuck.

The time spent in indecision, wavering from one thing to another, is usually spent talking ourselves out of what we know we really want, which is our heart-mind connection. Sometimes that feeling of frustration, of feeling stuck, could be your brain being challenged while you are pushing the boundaries of your comfort zone.

Perhaps some time ago you stopped believing in yourself and you stopped believing in possibility because of the disappointment you felt. Maybe as a child you had this idea that you couldn't trust anyone because somebody had let you down. Maybe it was a close family member, who lost your trust when they said they would do something and they didn't.

What has happened now is your brain is saying, "When I hope, I get disappointed. So what's the point in hoping anyway?" Perhaps while you're stuck, you're second-guessing and you're constantly doing your due diligence, weighing up all the options. You can't decide until you've looked at a hundred different options. But really it's a disguise for not trusting yourself. Your first instincts are usually right because your subconscious makes decisions before your conscious mind registers that there is a decision to be made.

A confused mind will always say no.

We have this dichotomy between what you know is right and what you are reasoning your way out of. Here's the truth: a confused mind will always say no, given too many options. When there are too many paths, your brain goes into self-preservation mode and says, "Nope, I'm not deciding. I would rather just stay where I am." Choosing feels like hard work because a confused mind stays in indecision. What happens is nothing is moving, and it results in frustration. Confusion is a result of the battle between the head and the heart. The heart wants what it wants, but the head is programmed to stay safe and avoid danger. It will warn you and say, "Don't take that path. The last time we did that, we got hurt," or, "We didn't like that, so let's not do that again."

We try to avoid disappointment by avoiding belief in ourselves, but what are we missing out on by not believing? Just think about it for a minute. What if you believe in yourself, you agree that you are capable, you are favored, you have everything you need, and things do go well for you? What if you accept that you are loved and that you are more than worthy enough to get what you're dreaming of? What if you started believing that?

The heart-mind connection is your heart, your gut, and your intuition. It's actually your spirit crying out to be connected to your mind. As people of faith, we know that the Holy Spirit resides within us, which is who we are at our core. Yet we have to work through the soulish part, which is our mind, our will, and our emotions. Our spirit and our soul are at odds with each other because our mind gets imprinted with past behaviors and thinking.

The Spirit is saying, "Maybe you can believe, maybe you can have faith, maybe you can step out." What you want to do is get back to listening to your heart and the Holy Spirit that lives inside of you. Just ask yourself this without any judgment: "Am I listening to my heart and spirit?" What is it saying? Does something come to mind that you've been thinking and dreaming of, that you wouldn't dare to say out loud? Consider this your opportunity to put it down on paper and to start digging into those areas to dig out the golden nuggets.

Here is the good news: even though your brain might be trying to stop you from advancing, you can retrain it. The brain is plastic and has the quality of neuroplasticity. No matter your past trauma, past experience, education, bias, or beliefs, your brain can be rewired for optimal performance.

Dr. Caroline Leaf, a well-known neuroscientist, says we are not a victim of the biology of our past experiences[32]. There's an increasing body of evidence that shows that the brain changes according to experience. Frequent positive and challenging learning experiences can actually increase intelligence in a relatively short amount of time.

The anatomy and physiology of the human brain is much more malleable and plastic than we once thought. The brain changes according to how we use it. That's great news! This means you're not stuck with the brain you were born with. You can rewire and retrain it to work at its optimum.

However, you need to trust the process. Rewiring your mind takes consistent effort to override your old programming. But it can be done!

Growth Is Like Grieving

I like to tell people that growth can feel like grieving when you are letting go of what you once held dear. Being in-between where you want to be, and where you are, is a very strange dichotomy. I like to call it the "messy middle." It's the in-between of letting go of something that you once valued as important, as you step into the unknown.

Growth can feel like grieving when you are letting go of what you once held dear.

Perhaps the old you felt that your fears and anxieties kept you safe, and you were comfortable with that. Now the new you is craving change, but your brain is going to fight you on the change. The toddler brain might say: "Wait, this is uncomfortable. Why are we giving this up? This feels sad. I don't want to move on. What is it going to be like out there?" It's taking that step of faith. You need to engage your therapist brain, and say to yourself: "It's okay, I'm safe, I can do this. There's no danger. You served me well, but now it's time to move on."

We all have thoughts running through our mind and we don't challenge them.

Are you willing and ready to do the work of rewiring your brain? A useful exercise is to take a pen and paper and ask yourself this question: "What limiting belief do I need to let go of to progress?" No idea or thought process is bad. All ideas are good. We want to be able to write them all down, get them out from our subconscious, and start to make them real.

We might feel like something has to change, but we don't know what to do to make the change. That inevitably leaves us feeling stuck. Sometimes we don't know what that limiting belief is, because we all have blind spots and we don't know what we don't know. I'm an optimistic realist. It's not always going to be sunshine, lollipops, and rainbows. Life is life; you have to take the good with the bad. But think about it for a minute, and ask yourself this: "If I didn't have any limits to my circumstances, my financial position, my relationship status, what would my life look like? What would I want my life to look like?"

We all experience daily doubts and the pressure of daily dramas. We have all lived through the crazy of 2020, and how that dramatically shifted our lives across the globe. The last time the world experienced a global crisis on those proportions was during World War II, which left ripples decades later. For the first time in this generation every single human on the planet felt the seismic shift of world events that shook up our daily routines and lives. For many individuals, the interruption to their lives came as a violent jolt, and accepting the change did not come easily.

How do we learn from our past experiences and turn them into good? It starts with a change in thinking. If we dwell on what once was our happy, comfortable place, and we pine for the old, then we will never fully embrace the new. This "stuckness" is not productive and will sour our confidence and outlook on life. Sometimes we are forced into change, and the best thing we can do for ourselves is to adapt and be ready to pivot. A big part of this process is learning to let go.

How do we build resilience and learn to rise above our circumstances? We deal with daily challenges, but how do we get above it and not feel like we are drowning ? How you do that is by taking control of your thoughts and owning your position as captain of your ship. You replace your toddler and teenager drama brain for the adult therapist brain who can think through things in a calm manner. A good train of thought is: "I have a choice here. I might have been programmed from my childhood to anticipate the worst or the negative, but I can change my stuck story." Just knowing that it is possible enables your brain to reach for something beyond what it sees right now.

> *Just knowing that it is possible enables your brain to reach for something beyond what it sees right now.*

The concept of the 5 Whys was coined by Taiichi Ohno of the Toyota Motor Corporation[33]. He had a system of working with his employees to get to the perfect answer. His idea is that you keep asking "Why?" five times. When we do that, we get under the hood of realizing the real reason behind a problem.

The way your brain works is through modeling or mirroring. When you see somebody else being coached on a topic, often it feels like something that you've experienced yourself. Seeing somebody else overcome a challenge actually helps you to train your brain to apply the same principles. If somebody is having an issue with something, and you see them come to an awareness, then it's like a light bulb goes off in your mind too.

So challenge yourself today to think about your limiting beliefs, even if it's just one limiting belief and write it down. Ask yourself: "Why do I think that? When did I start thinking that? Why did I believe that? Was it based on truth or perception or what I was taught? What behaviors were modeled to me?"

We all come with junk in our trunk from our childhood. This is your opportunity to start to retrain your mind and behavior and to reform, so that whatever you are destined for tomorrow, you can achieve.

Self-Reflection Exercise

- Reflect and stand back as you look at yourself objectively.
- Separate your "who" (your identity) from your "do" (your actions or habits).
- Do you see the need to change? Why?
- Can you trace the origin of that limiting belief or toxic habit?
- Reflect and think about an alternate belief that you can replace it with.

13

Stop the Self-Sabotage

"If you don't believe in yourself, somewhere or another, you sabotage yourself."
Jason Day

Do you ever feel you're your own worst enemy? Like you're doing everything you can to sabotage your own success? This is a common problem, and it's called self-sabotage. Our brain is always seeking comfort. When we push against the comfort boundaries by doing something new or scary, it causes either a fight, flight, freeze, or fawn response. This primitive brain response would have served to keep us safe back when we were running away from hungry lions, but we're not doing that anymore.

The issue is never the issue; there is always something more that is the underlying issue. We need to dig deep to find out what is really going on behind the scenes if we are to truly find freedom. But first, we need to stop self-sabotaging!

Dr. Marsha Linehan[34] is the creator of dialectical behavior therapy (DBT)[35]. She says, "Shame is your mortal enemy. Shame makes you hide. You're not going to be able to help yourself, because you're so ashamed that you're hiding from yourself."

What Is Self-Sabotage?

Self-sabotage is an actual thing. We have all probably experienced it in our lives. Sometimes we do it without even realizing it. We may think that we are doing ourselves a favor by not trying, or by sabotaging our own efforts. Self-sabotage only leads to unhappiness and regret. There are many ways that people sabotage their own lives, but the result is always the same: disappointment and frustration.

Anything new is a challenge to our brain, and we become self-critical when we don't have all the answers. This results in postponing making decisions by making excuses. Excuses are a means of delaying getting down to business, and the saboteur likes to find any excuse not to move forward.

Slowing down may seem cumbersome and inconvenient, yet it is necessary to slow down to accelerate your progress. So if you want to discover what the root of the issue is, you need to be willing to push yourself to the edge of your comfort zone, and stop your brain from freaking out!

Identity and Self-Sabotage

If you don't have a healthy self-concept, you're not going to want to put yourself out there and take risks. I come from a classically trained ballet background, and I'm also an adult figure skater. With my keen interest in sports psychology, I love to ask, "How do I overcome the moments when I'm challenging my brain and my body to do something new while pushing against my comfort zones?"

It's about getting to a place where you feel calm, cool, and collected and you're making decisions out of forethought—versus feeling like you're chasing this never-ending pinata that is flying around your head that you can't see.

What we are dealing with is habitual habits and patterns that have got you where you are today. How do we undo that? How do we go back and rebuild your self-concept? How do we redefine who you are, and how you want to show up in the world?

Women especially are very hard on themselves. We are very self-critical, and our fear holds us back from making decisions. We can't make sound business, life, and relational decisions from a lack of self-sabotage. We want to make a decision and move forward, but we find ourselves nitpicking things and finding holes or excuses. Excuses are a delay tactic for getting down to business and doing the work under the hood.

> *The problem is never the problem. There is always a root issue that we're dealing with that holds us back.*

Lack of awareness of the problem is a big part of the problem. Unless you come to that realization and say, "I have a problem," you cannot move forward. Not everybody is ready to do the important work. People want to be in denial because ignorance is bliss. That's cool—until something happens. It's usually when the wheels fall off the bus, or some change happens like they lose money, or a relationship goes sour. It is when they have a tipping point they come to the realization that, "I cannot do this any more."

How to Stop Self-Sabotage

If you're ready to stop self-sabotaging and start achieving your goals, follow these seven steps, and you'll be well on your way to success!

1. Identify your self-sabotaging behaviors

Have you had issues with procrastination and making excuses? Do you allow your fear of failure to hold you back? Once you know what your self-sabotaging behaviors are, you can work on changing them. Without awareness, you won't know what to work on. As much as we would like to ignore it, denial is no longer an option!

2. Understand why you self-sabotage

What are the underlying reasons? Are you afraid of success? Do you have low self-esteem? Once you understand the root cause of your self-sabotage, you can work on changing your mindset. However, if you believe that you're not good enough, or that you'll never be successful, then it's time to change your thoughts. Think about when you first started thinking this way. Was it from childhood, or a terrible experience? Start thinking positive things about yourself, and creating the self-belief that you can accomplish anything you set your mind to. Believe that it is done before it is done, because that is how failure faith works. Have the belief that no matter how many times you fail, you will have the faith to continue.

3. Set realistic goals

Don't try to bite off more than you can chew. Try to start small and gradually increase the difficulty of your goals as you gain confidence. Set realistic goals for yourself and make a plan to achieve them. Don't accomplish too much at once, or you'll become overwhelmed and discouraged. Break your goals down into small, manageable pieces, and focus on one thing at a time.

4. Develop a positive self-image

Believe in yourself and your ability to achieve your goals. This isn't a cliche; without self-belief you won't take the steps to change your mindset. Entertaining defeating thoughts only adds to the list of self-sabotaging behaviors. Remember: you are the only one who can hold yourself back!

5. Get rid of negative self-talk

Whenever you have a negative thought about yourself, exchange it for a positive one. For example, if you think, "I'm not good enough," tell yourself, "I am good enough." I like to call it going on a "negativity talk fast" to censor your speech. In the same way, if you spent years talking negatively about yourself, you're going to put in the same effort to talk positively about yourself. Our brain will believe repeating patterns, so it's important you make this shift.

6. Take action

Set your goals, believe in yourself, and then take action towards achieving them. Don't let self-sabotage stand in your way any longer! Comparatively, if you don't take action today, nothing will change tomorrow. You have the power to create the life you want, so go out there and do it!

7. Surround yourself with positive people

Find others who will support and encourage you. These people will help you stay motivated, and they'll be there to celebrate your successes with you. Although you may feel you're alone in these areas of struggle, know that self-sabotage is very common. Equally important is filtering your environment and what you watch and listen to. Remember: the eyes are the window to the soul! You will believe what you hear and see as a result of your inputs.

In conclusion, if you're struggling with self-sabotage, remember that you're not alone. Many people struggle with this issue. But if you're willing to work on it, you can overcome self-sabotage and achieve success! Just take it one step at a time and remember not to give up on yourself. You've got this!

Self-Reflection Exercise

- What self-sabotaging behaviors do you exhibit when you are confronted with the fear of failure or success?
- What small step can you take to move toward your goals irrespective if it feels hard or challenging?
- What personally motivating belief statement can you start using to rewire your brain?

14

Fixed versus Growth Mindset

"Everyone grows but not everyone becomes mature."
Kemi Sogunle

Have you ever felt like you're not good enough? Like no matter what you do, you can't seem to achieve your goals? If so, you're not alone. Many people struggle with self-confidence and low self-esteem. The good news is that there is a solution: your mindset. It is the driver of everything in your life.

As people of faith, we know that we are born for a reason and for a season and by design. If we can tap into that, and align our minds with our hearts and our intuition spirit, then everything else falls in place. I think this is one of the most underrated aspects of healthcare.

Why Mindset Is the Key

Mindset is the collection of thoughts, beliefs, and attitudes that you have about yourself and the world. It shapes how you see yourself and how you interact with others. Carol Dweck[36], Professor of Psychology at Stanford University and author of *Mindset: The New Psychology of Success*[37], says your mindset can be positive or negative; you can have a fixed or a growth mindset[38].

Fixed versus Growth Mindset

Carol Dweck studies human motivation and why some people succeed where others don't. Her theory is based on two mindsets—fixed and growth, and the difference they make in the outcomes in people's lives. Her book takes us on a journey into how our conscious and unconscious thoughts affect us, as well as how something as simple as wording can have a powerful impact on our ability to improve.

Carol Dweck says:

> The passion for stretching yourself and sticking to it, even (or especially) when it's not going well, is the hallmark of the growth mindset. This is the mindset that allows people to thrive during some of the most challenging times in their lives. I've seen so many people with this one consuming goal of proving themselves—in the classroom, in their careers, and in their relationships.

Carol Dweck goes on to talk about mindset as a basis for cultivating growth:

> Every situation calls for a confirmation of their intelligence, personality, or character. Every situation is evaluated: Will I succeed or fail? Will I look smart or dumb? Will I be accepted or rejected? Will I feel like a winner or a loser? There's another mindset in which these traits are not simply a hand you're dealt and have to live with, always trying to convince yourself and others that you have a royal flush when you're secretly worried it's a pair of tens. In this mindset, the hand you're dealt is just the starting point for development. This growth mindset is based on the belief that your basic qualities are things you can cultivate through your efforts.

A Fixed Mindset

If you have a fixed mindset, you're likely to give up when things get tough. Or you may not even try at all, because you don't believe you can succeed. You may struggle with feelings of inadequacy and insecurity. It can also prevent you from taking valuable risks or trying new things because you're afraid of failing. A fixed mindset is one in which you believe your skills and abilities are set in stone, because of your past experiences or failures. You may think you're not smart enough or talented enough to achieve your goals. This can lead to feelings of hopelessness and helplessness.

A Growth Mindset

By comparison, a growth mindset is one where you believe you can develop your skills and abilities. You understand that effort and practice are keys to success. This mindset leads to increased motivation and resilience in the face of setbacks.

Carol Dweck says:

> In a growth mindset, people believe that their most basic abilities can be developed through dedication and hard work—brains and talent are just the starting point. This view creates a love of learning and a resilience that is essential for great accomplishment.

During your life you can expect to face challenges that question your mental grit and resilience. With a growth mindset, you're more likely to persevere through challenges, versus falling apart at the first sign of difficulty. You'll also be more open to feedback and willing to put in the work needed to improve your productivity.

Am I Open to Change?

To kick start the process ask yourself these questions: Am I teachable? Am I able to open myself up to learn new things? Am I coachable? Am I open to learning, even if it means being open to failure?

The good news is that anyone can change if they put their mind to it. You can cultivate a growth mindset by being aware, and by being intentional with your thoughts and actions. If we can apply hope and agency within a growth mindset, we can access the tools and power and set goals with hope for a real outcome. It is important to understand that some systems in society are oppressive. Changing on your own is hard! This is where as believers we can equip, cultivate and empower the next generation. We need to help each other to identify the tools and access them using a team "we are one body" approach.

Self-Reflection Exercise

- What lies or distractions are keeping you from taking action?
- What fixed-minded thoughts can you choose to challenge or ignore?
- What is one thing you can focus on today to help you take a small step forward?

15

Fixed to Flexibility

"You may not control all the events that happen to you, but you can decide not to be reduced by them."
Dr. Maya Angelou

When we are stuck in a cocoon, we often don't see the benefits of a change, says Dr. Kelly McGonigal, health psychologist and lecturer at Stanford University. Even if we were to engage in that change, we might not see the benefits straightaway. Instead, we need to think about the long-term benefits of making a change. Things might seem fine now, but if you were to push outside your habits or your comfort zone, something really positive could flourish. It's very easy not to look for the thing that would take us to the next level. The key to getting unstuck is to identify what the change will be. One of the best ways to put yourself in a position to see what your opportunities are, is to be very connected to your own values.

"When people are connected to their values, they actually get much better at being receptive to messages that there's something they can do that would really be of benefit to them." says Dr. Kelly McGonigal.

People instinctively gravitate toward being receptive to information about how it supports their own well-being. You're unable to see the opportunities that are available. Just being connected to your own values makes you less likely to get stuck.

Think of it like a stress mindset reset and barometer test. When you first start to notice stress arising, if your tendency is to shut down, avoid, or distract yourself, then first recognize what you're feeling. Your emotional response is a signal that something you care about is at stake. Stress and anxiety can be good for you when you understand that they are not illnesses or disabilities to be avoided, but signals. They are biological responses and warning signals that need your attention.

Stress and anxiety can be good for you when you understand that they are not illnesses or disabilities to be avoided, but signals. Changing the meaning of that signal is how you allow the emotional state not to debilitate you. A good practice is to ask yourself, "What do I care about? Who do I care about? Why do I care?"

Studies show that in moments of any sort of distress or discomfort, as soon as people reflect on what they care about, it changes what is going on biologically. Allowing yourself to calmly process an uncomfortable emotion reduces stress, inflammation, or cortisol, and increases motivation in the brain.

Remember the Why

Simon Sinek's book *Start with Why* took the world by storm when it opened up our minds to the question, "Why am I doing this?" Remembering your "Why" is a powerful motivator when you find yourself tempted by a challenge. If a recovering alcoholic is tempted to drink, being reminded of their "why" for changing (like their family) can change their behavior. They don't need some outside influence to tell them why over-drinking is bad for their health; if they're internally motivated to change based on their why, then that change will stick. People will do whatever it takes if they really care about it.

People will do whatever it takes if they really care about it.

It's about changing the meaning of discomfort, stress, or pain. You learn to understand that it is the signal to think about why you care. When you are fully expectant that discomfort is part of life, you can embrace stress as a signal when you need to course correct. Instead of fearing or avoiding the feelings of anxiety, you can learn from your biological and emotional responses that, "Oh, that's a signal, I had better course correct. I need to get back in alignment with my values." Think about the process and what story you will tell yourself about why you care, and why this change is meaningful to you.

Dr. McGonigal goes on to say that the default mode of the brain is to be critical and comparative, rather than values-driven or self-reflective. Values affirmation works because you're shifting out of that default brain state. When you're in it, it's so hard to get out of your habit. Your brain's autopilot is engaged when you're not focused on something else. When you can connect with the more expansive, connected, and transcendent version of yourself, then you're getting out of the default mode.

Clarifying Values

Dr. Dan Siegel says that when we're clarifying our values, it brings us out of an egocentric perspective of, "I need this discomfort to go away. I want a supportive environment right now." It's taking the attention off yourself and your feelings, and placing value on what is really important to you. This becomes an external motivation to help keep you motivated to move toward the change. Your higher values are what really matter to you. They are what connect you to others in a meaningful way. They are what connect you to nature or the work that you're doing for the greater good, or your family, or your friends. It is also why faith and a belief in a higher power is so valuable to your mental and emotional health. Believing in something or someone bigger helps put things into perspective. It is also the basis for hope, because without hope, the human spirit deteriorates.

Dr. Siegel goes on to say:

It's similar to the way that gratitude holds up so well in the research on well-being. Gratitude works because if you're being grateful in the moment, you're letting go of the preoccupation of the immediate desire. Gratitude is almost always gratitude for something outside of ourselves. This kind of connection to outside meaning defuses all of our instinctual self-preservation impulses that get us into so much trouble.

I like to say that you can't be grateful and grumpy at the same time! It's about noticing that the cup is half full rather than half empty.

Valuing Your Values

Dr. Jennifer Crocker, PhD, a psychologist at Ohio State University[39], says that thinking about your values puts you in a different emotional state. Her studies on self-esteem revealed that people who base their self-worth on what others think, and not on their intrinsic value as human beings, might pay a mental and physical price.

Her research appeared in an issue of the Journal of Social Issues (Vol. 58, No. 3) in 2002 Dr. Crocker surveyed more than six hundred college freshmen three times during the year: before they left for college, and at the end of the fall and spring semesters. What the study found was that college students who based their self-worth on external sources, like appearance, approval from others, and academic performance, reported more stress, anger, academic problems, and relationship conflicts. They had higher levels of drug and alcohol abuse and symptoms of eating disorders. Despite being highly motivated and studying more hours each week, students who based their self-worth on academic outcomes were also more likely to report conflicts with professors and greater stress. Dr. Crocker speculated that students who base their self-worth on academic performance might become anxious and distracted, feel threatened by feelings of failure, and have their anxiety interfere with their memory.

Students who based their self-esteem on internal motivations, such as being a virtuous person or adhering to moral standards, were found to achieve higher grades. They were less likely to use alcohol and drugs or to develop eating disorders. Dr. Crocker found that after thinking about personal values, these students reported feeling more connected, more empathetic, more hopeful, and more humble. That is the self who can make a change: the self who feels both humble and hopeful at the same time.

Dr. Crocker said:

> We really think that if people could adopt goals not focused on their own self-esteem but on something larger than their self—such as what they can create or contribute to others—than they would be less susceptible, to some of the negative effects of pursuing self-esteem. It's about having a goal that is bigger than the self.

Escaping Stuckness

Dr. Joan Borysenko says that we get stuck about "stuckness." There is a poem called "Usai" by Roger Keyes. "Usai" is short for "Hokusai," who was a famous Japanese artist. One of my favorite lines from the poem is: "He says get stuck, accept it, repeat yourself as long as it's interesting."

Ask yourself, "Is this behavior pattern still interesting to me?" People do get over being stuck when it stops being interesting. Give yourself permission to be stuck, and then give yourself permission to let it pass through. This is encouraging you to change in a compassionate way.

Self-Reflection Exercise

Let's do a values intervention and answer these questions. Examples of values are family, faith, freedom, politics, social justice, creativity, compassion, fun, adventure, etc. Come up with what is valuable to you.

- What do I really care about in life?
- What are my most important values?
- What do I want to do in the next couple of weeks that would support my goals and my well-being?
- Is there anything that I might be interested in doing or trying?

Now think about one that feels personally meaningful to you:

- Why did I choose that value?
- Why did I choose that value as an important value?
- How does that show up in my everyday life?
- How has that value supported me?

16

Pushing Through Boundaries

"There is freedom waiting for you, On the breezes of the sky, And you ask 'What if I fall?' Oh but my darling, What if you fly?"
Erin Hanson

Our desire to avoid pain can put us in a cocoon and make us feel stuck. Our brains are hardwired to avoid discomfort, and to get unstuck requires being comfortable with discomfort. The process of breaking free from what is keeping you stuck often requires experiencing feelings like anxiety, self-doubt, or physical discomfort. When we meet that first point of discomfort, we may think that it would be easier to remain the same rather than to push on. Getting unstuck is a process of finding a way to embrace the discomfort when we first start trying to get out of the cocoon. Just like a caterpillar ready to evolve into a butterfly, at first living in the cocoon can feel very nice and cozy. Only when the caterpillar has outgrown the cocoon does it feel limited.

The breakthrough usually comes when you have hit rock bottom, and you're more sick and tired of whatever is keeping you stuck. When you get to the point of, "I don't want this anymore," then you are ready to break free from the cocoon and do whatever it takes to escape.

If you haven't reached that stage yet, it's very important to determine what you don't want any more. Dr. Kelly McGonigal talks about the "Missing Zero

Strategy."[40] It is something that you'll be giving up if you say yes or no to this thing. For example, it's the thing that you lose when you say yes to the cookie. When you say no to the cookie, you are choosing the health benefits. You are giving up the immediate gratification of the taste of the cookie, in place of a healthy body–that's the missing zero.

What Are the Costs of Staying the Same?

Sometimes people just don't know the answer because of the fear of the unknown. You walk through a door, and it often opens up to other doors. But from behind the initial door, you don't really know what it might open. Taking an opportunity that you might fail is a step of faith.

Think of it this way: so what if you fail? What are your real losses and gains? Would it be that bad if you actually just tried? Taking a step and moving forward can create momentum. Even if you pick the wrong choice, just by making a choice you will know whether that choice was right or wrong for you in the first place. Knowing what you don't want is just as important as knowing what you do want.

Knowing what you don't want is just as important as knowing what
you do want.

When you avoid something because you want to avoid the pain, discomfort, or self-doubt, what you actually experience is disappointment, frustration, and a feeling of stagnation. You feel the cost of avoidance immediately. You've just swapped one set of uncomfortable feelings for another.

It's a paradox. We resist or avoid making a change or taking action. If we avoid the motivation or reason behind inaction, then we actually end up strengthening the experience we want to avoid!

For example, maybe you don't want to risk getting hurt by going on a date to find a relationship. What you end up with is feelings of isolation, loneliness, or feeling unloved. Often it's the very kind of experience that you're trying to defend or protect yourself against! So what are you actually choosing by choosing or not choosing?

It's the same if you are stuck feeling anxious; you are choosing not to do something. You want to avoid the feelings of fear and anxiety. This is one of the reasons why avoiding discomfort becomes a cycle. It is because we are so afraid of feeling the discomfort. What we don't realize is that we're much more capable of tolerating it thank we think.

Pain Tolerance

A study[41] called the "Personal values and pain tolerance: does a value intervention add to acceptance?" was conducted to test if "Acceptance interventions based upon Acceptance and Commitment Therapy (ACT)"[42] would show a greater tolerance of acute pain. ACT was developed in the 1980s by psychologist Steven C. Hayes, a professor at the University of Nevada. He said:

> We as a culture seem to be dedicated to the idea that "negative" human emotions need to be fixed, managed, or changed—not experienced as part of a whole life. We are treating our own lives as problems to be solved, as if we can sort through our experiences for the ones we like and throw out the rest. Acceptance, mindfulness and values are key psychological tools needed for that transformative shift[43].

The ACT process[44] is an action-oriented approach to psychotherapy that stems from traditional behavior and cognitive therapy. A patient learns to stop avoiding, denying, and struggling with their emotions. Instead, they learn to accept that these deeper feelings are appropriate responses to certain situations. They discover that emotions should not stop them from moving forward in their lives. Once understood, patients begin to accept their hardships as part of life and commit to making necessary changes in their behavior. They learn to push through the pain regardless of what is going on in their lives, and they learn how to process and deal with their feelings.

Once we "break through" to the other side of pain, we find that we have overcome and are now stronger and more capable of handling future challenges. This is building your emotional muscle of maturity and resilience. You build your pain tolerance by telling yourself, "This may be uncomfortable now, but I can handle it."

It's so important to know what your big "Why" is behind any sort of change or challenge that will involve discomfort. Being so afraid of feeling discomfort is only going to keep you stuck in the cocoon. It's only when you start stretching, pushing, and enduring that you discover what you're truly capable of. A perfect example is a mother going through childbirth. She knows that the process is going to be painful, but each contraction is bringing her closer to meeting her newborn, so she endures. She pushes through the pain because the gain or reward far outweighs the temporary pain and discomfort. Pain is not avoided but embraced as a necessary part of the process. When you imagine that the pain that you're feeling is in service of a value that you care about, you will surprise yourself with how much you can handle.

Strategy of Mindfulness and Acceptance

Here is a great visualization technique I like to refer to as "stepping off the edge of the ledge." Let's get uncomfortable for a moment. Let's see what arises in your body as you tune into your senses. Think about what it would feel like once you've already made the decision. Allow yourself to feel the discomfort, anxiety, and fear. Remember that you have complete freedom at this moment. Learning how to tolerate discomfort is a crucial element of developing emotional maturity. It's a powerful tool to allow your mind and body to move through the negative emotions, without them becoming debilitating. Through this process you have learned how to overcome and break through the fears, anxiety, and discomfort by facing them head on.

Think of it like going to the dentist. Nobody likes to have an injection or have their teeth pulled, but we know dental health is a necessary part of life. For children, the anticipation of the event is far worse than the event itself. They get so worked up about the size of the needle or the fear of the unknown, they can cause themselves distress. As a parent of three now grown kids, I can attest that talking them through what it would actually feel like, and reminding them of the greater reward on the other side, gave them the fortitude to endure.

> *"Those who trust in the Lord are like Mount Zion, which cannot be shaken but endures forever."*
> *Psalm 125:1, NIV*

Future Projections

It's important to know what the positive vision is for the future to help you reach for your ultimate goal. Dr. Dan Siegel[45] talks about how all distress, emotional as well as physical, is a series of moment-to-moment bodily sensations. Allowing yourself to feel and move through the sensations is how you objectively process the mind-body messages that your feelings are sending your brain.

Asking yourself questions like, "What does it feel like to be anxious in this way?" and then take note of how it feels in your body. Then move onto, "When the anxiety drops down and decreases, how does it feel then?" You want to focus on the future as if you are already there, having gone through the anxiety and are now on the other side. Think of it like you're creating a positive future with this positive expectancy language.

It's called "presupposition," where you presuppose that the change is going to happen. We can train ourselves to talk in presupposition of the future that we hope for. It's pulling you into that positive vision of your ideal future.

Opportunity Loss Self-Reflection Exercise

- Is there anything in your life that you would like to do or pursue or change, but that you're not doing because of how stressful or difficult it feels?
- What are you losing out on when you refuse to do something that would

help you change or pursue a goal that is important to you?

- Are there any opportunities that you have not said yes to in the past, and what were the costs of that?
- What are the costs of saying no to an opportunity because you aren't 100 percent sure you'll succeed or that you can handle it?
- Is there something you're putting off because you just don't want to face how it feels now, when you think about having to actually get it done?
- Would it enrich your life in any way if you were able to make that choice?
- What are the costs of choosing not to take that next step?
- What are the costs of choosing to stay the same?
- What are the costs of saying no?
- What are you missing out on or losing?
- If you were in the same position a year, five, and ten years from now, how would you feel?
- Do you trust yourself enough to make the right choice?

17

How to Develop a Resilient Mindset

"Man never made any material as resilient as the human spirit."
Bernard Williams

During a study at Johns Hopkins in the 1950s, Dr. Curt Richter conducted a famous psychological experiment involving drowning rats. This experiment, albeit cruel, was designed to test the power of hope and resilience in overcoming difficult situations. The experiments began with placing twelve domesticated rats in a bucket of water to test how long they could tread water. Initially, the first of these rats swam around the surface, then dove to the bottom of the bucket to explore. This lasted two minutes before it drowned. Another two of the domesticated rats behaved the same way and survived for roughly the same time, hypothesizing learned behavior. The other nine domesticated rats did something different. After an initial exploration of the bottom of the bucket, they spent most of their time at the surface and just kept swimming. These nine survived for days before eventually succumbing to exhaustion and drowning.

Hope Is the Power of Resilience

The second set of experiments Dr. Curt Richter undertook involved thirty-four wild rats, who were excellent swimmers. With their savage and aggressive behavior, Dr. Richter presumed they would fight hard for their survival. Not a single one of the thirty-four wild rats survived more than a few minutes. Dr. Richter reflected on what caused some rats to give up, and he decided that hope was a key factor in the willingness to struggle on.

He said: "The situation of these rats scarcely seems one demanding fight or flight—it is rather one of hopelessness … the rats are in a situation against which they have no defense … they seem literally to 'give up.'"

The last set of experiments Dr. Richter tried were to test if, by introducing hope, the rats could increase their survival times. To test his hypothesis, Dr. Richter selected a new group of similar rats. Once again, he placed them into buckets and observed how they progressed. This time, though, at the moment at which each rat was about to give up, he intervened. He rescued them from the bucket, held them for a while, and helped them recover. He then placed the rats back into the buckets and started the experiments all over again.

What he discovered was that his hypothesis about hope was right. The rats that had been helped in the past, and had the hope of being saved, kept fighting. Once they were placed back into the water, they swam and swam for much longer than they had initially. The only difference was that they had hope from being saved before. When they believed that all hope was not lost, their will to survive outlasted their learned behavior.

Curt wrote, "The rats quickly learn that the situation is not actually hopeless," and that, "After elimination of hopelessness the rats do not die."

Even though rats and humans are different beings, what we can learn from this experiment is that hope has the power to fuel resilience. When an individual has hope, they have higher levels of perseverance, resilience, and grit. The hope of survival will keep them fighting when they know that there is a chance of success or rescue. When they don't have hope, they give up and die.

Faced with difficulty, humans will remain resilient and persevere—provided they have hope. If supported and rescued them from time to time, they will continue pushing through.

Dr. Richter said:

> The situation of these rats scarcely seems one demanding fight or flight—it is rather one of hopelessness; whether they are restrained in the hand or confined in the swimming jar, the rats are in a situation against which they have no defense. This reaction of hopelessness is shown by some wild rats very soon after being grasped in the hand and prevented from moving; they seem literally to "give up.

He went on to explain the introduction of hope:

> Support for the assumption that the sudden death phenomenon depends largely on emotional reactions to restraint or immersion comes from the observation that after elimination of the hopelessness the rats do not die. This is achieved by repeatedly holding the rats briefly and then freeing them, and by immersing them in water for a few minutes on several occasions. In this way, the rats quickly learn that the situation is not actually hopeless; thereafter they again become aggressive, try to escape, and show no signs of giving up. Wild rats so conditioned swim just as long as domestic rats or longer.

If we believe the future will be a better place for everyone, and if we feel others are there to help us, we can endure through difficult situations. The moral of the story is to just keep swimming and never give up! You might surprise yourself with what you can achieve. We all face challenges and obstacles daily. No one said that life would be easy. It's how we deal with these challenges that determine our success in life. Developing a resilient mindset is the key to overcoming challenges and seeing opportunities.

What Is a Resilient Mindset?

Resiliency is the ability to adapt to challenging situations. When stress arises, adversity strikes, or you experience trauma, you will experience anger, grief, and pain. But you're able to keep functioning (both physically and psychologically) and endure the challenges. Being resilient means that instead of falling into the pit of despair, or hiding from issues with unhealthy coping strategies, you face these difficulties straight on.

What Does It Mean to Be Resilient?

Developing a resilient mindset is one of the most important things you can do for yourself. It is key to overcoming any obstacle. When life throws challenges your way, it's essential to have the inner strength to keep going. Obstacles are going to come up, but with the right attitude, you can break through them and continue on your path. Most often, this includes giving up a victim mentality. This keeps you feeling like situations are beyond your control, that you don't have agency over your decisions, or that life is "out to get you." Similarly, in a professional setting, being resilient can reduce your risk of burnout.

What Are the Seven Resilience Skills?

According to Dr. Kenneth Ginsburg, child pediatrician and human development expert, there are seven integral and interrelated components that make up being resilient. They include "competence, confidence, connection, character, contribution, coping," as well as control. For instance, optimism has shown to help soften the impact of stress on the mind, as well as on the body, because of disturbing experiences.

How to Develop a Resilient Mindset

There are many factors that determine resilience. Things like genetics, early childhood experiences, and circumstances can't be changed. But it is possible to learn specific skills to build resilience, as long as you are open to change. These include breaking out of negative thought patterns and cycles, habits, and behaviors. It also includes resisting the urge to catastrophize events (like being a drama queen), and looking for the upside of life when faced with setbacks. By the same token, we undervalue the importance of seeing challenges as resilience building exercises.

The Keys to Unlocking a Resilient Mindset

- See challenges as opportunities, not obstacles.
- Don't give up so easily when things get tough.
- Remember that persistence is key.
- Have determination.
- See the bright side of every situation.
- Remain focused on your goals.
- Challenges strengthen us, so embrace them.
- Develop a positive mindset.
- Surround yourself with positive people.
- Believe in yourself.
- Know when to give up and walk away.
- Overcome challenges one step at a time.
- Don't be afraid to ask for help.
- Practice gratitude.
- Meditate and pray regularly.
- Learn from your mistakes.
- Focus on solutions, not problems.
- Have faith in God and trust in His plan for your life.

We now know that resilient individuals don't let difficulties, traumatic experiences, or failure overcome them and drain their resolve. Instead, the highly resilient change their course, dig deep to heal emotionally, and continue moving toward their goals and dreams. No matter what life throws your way, use these eighteen mental hacks to help you develop a resilient mindset. You will be well on your way to overcoming any challenge that comes your way!

Self-Reflection Exercise

- Are you thinking like a victim in any area of your life?
- What difficult thing are you avoiding?
- How can you flip the narrative on a challenge you are currently experiencing by seeing the positive in this situation?

18

Unlock Possibility Thinking

"I think anything is possible if you have the mindset and the will and desire to do it and put the time in."
Roger Clemens

My ten-year-old daughter loved catching fireflies on hot summer nights. She loved watching them fly around in the back garden, especially when their "bums" would glow. She was having fun catching them gently, placing them in a glass jar, and watching them trying to escape. She soon realized that it would be cruel to keep them cooped up in the jar with limited oxygen, since it was not their natural habitat. Being the animal lover that she is, she quickly released them. As she was playing with this mason jar with its wiggly lid, I thought to myself, "How much does the jar actually contain?" If you think about it, with its lid closed, the capacity is limited to its internal volume. How much water or sand or bugs that could be contained in a single jar is limited.

Your mind and your heart are jars for containment, but you are the one who puts a lid on your capacity. When you open up the lid, the capacity is expanded. How much volume can it contain now? When you have the lid closed (and your brain is like the jar), it is limited. We were taught as children to fill it to capacity with everything from education, to language, to cultural norms, beliefs, and behaviors.

What if you took the lid off and allowed yourself to be filled from different places? When you open the lid, you expand your capacity by opening yourself up to infinite possibilities. You come to know what you don't know. When you become an open vessel, you contain what is greater than yourself. You are open to absorbing and being open to opportunity. You become open to being expanded upon, because there are no limits when you remove the lid. The truth is there is always something greater than our current knowledge and understanding. Only an open vessel and an open heart can contain the infinity of life. This is possibility thinking.

What Is Possibility?

As an adult, I've learned to challenge the limits to my capacity when I have placed a lid on my potential. It has to occur within us first that there are limits to our current viewpoint. It's like the light bulb moment has to come on, knowing that it is possible to achieve. To achieve big things, you first need to visualize big things.

> *"And then GOD answered: 'Write this. Write what you see. Write it out in big block letters so that it can be read on the run. This vision-message is a witness pointing to what's coming. It aches for the coming—it can hardly wait! And it doesn't lie. If it seems slow in coming, wait. It's on its way. It will come right on time.'"*
> *Habakkuk 2:2-3, MSG*

When you have a vision and you make a plan to execute the vision, believing that it is possible is what fires up your soul. Believing that it is possible gets you pretty much 80 percent of the way there. If I look at the stories of professional athletes and those who are high achievers, one thing they do really, really well is they know how to get into possibility thinking. They visualize, they imagine themselves winning, they embody the feelings, and they get visceral. Just like Tiger Woods who thinks through and visualizes every shot, or like Michael Jordan the basketball player. They imagine themselves standing on the podium winning. You can practice winning in your mind before it actually happens. You don't have to wait for the circumstances to appear first; that is what faith is all about—believing before seeing. When you embrace possibility thinking, there is no need to self-sabotage anymore, because you will finally get out of your own way!

Imagine you want to achieve a goal. How you make it possible is by thinking, dreaming, and writing about it. Embrace possibility by feeling it in your body, and imagine what it will be like taking the steps. You are rehearsing the choreography of the dance of success in your mind so when it comes time to step up and perform, you already know what to do. When you really focus on achieving what you want to achieve, it doesn't seem insurmountable, because you've already imagined it is possible. What is possible can be done!

I know this can be a little bit of a brain twister, but stay with me. The mind is the driver of your vehicle. Your mind drives the results and the circumstances in your life. You need to come out of the fog of thinking that it has to stay this way. You don't need concrete proof to know that it is possible to achieve. This can be a challenge for logician personalities who need irrefutable proof, data, and statistics before they will take a step forward. Requiring too much analysis and proof before making decisions is only going to result in analysis paralysis, which is going to keep you stuck.

Shifting Realities

What if you challenge yourself to step out in faith and embrace possibility thinking? When you partner with God in stepping out, you are guaranteed to have a safety net, so what is there to lose? Once you know that every action and result and circumstance comes from a thought, and you're able to take your thoughts captive, then you start to realize infinite possibilities. When you let go of your current reality to embrace new realities, based on possibilities, you are shifting realities. In other words, there are no limits!

Many people live their lives inside their comfort zone. What if you pushed yourself out a little further, so you could breach the current boundaries of your potential ? What if you went over the hill, around the horizon, and discovered something new? How we do this is by practicing the thought that anything is possible.

> *"Jesus replied, 'What is impossible with man is possible with God.'"*
> *Luke 18:27, NIV*

This is pivotal and integral to faith. Our atheist friends would say, "I don't believe it because there isn't any indisputable proof." As believing Christians, we must have faith in a God we don't see. We don't have visual proof that He is here, but the proof does arrive as we live and as we breathe because we are in Him, and He is in us. If you can stay in faith, imagine how much you can achieve when you put faith in yourself and in God, and allow yourself to think that anything is possible!

Breaking Records

Here is a prime example. Sir Roger Bannister[46] was an English middle-distance athlete and a neurologist. He ran the first sub-four-minute mile on May 6, 1954, in three minutes and 59.4 seconds. It was a Guinness World Record, which had not been broken in nine years. Yet just forty-six days later, on June 21, 1954, Bannister's record was broken by his rival, John Landy, with a time of three minutes and 57.9 seconds. If you think about it, why did it take so many years for a runner to break the record? And yet just forty-six days later it was broken again? John Landy embraced possibility thinking because he saw Roger Bannister achieve it. He saw that it was possible for a long-standing record to be broken, so the limitations to his jar of potential was taken off. Today, to run a sub-four minute mile is not a big deal, because the bar of excellence has been raised by every individual who believes in possibility thinking.

My husband is a marathon runner, so I asked him about this. Roger had to have faith in himself first, to know that he could achieve the impossible. Roger had to put in the training and practice to perform at that pace, but also keeping in mind that it was achievable. He had believed it was attainable before it was accomplished. Perhaps what went on in John's head was to imagine that it was possible by modeling Roger's winning behavior. Then it became true and inevitable.

He had believed it was attainable before it was accomplished.

When we see others breaking barriers and achieving big things, it gives our brains proof of possibility. When it has been done, it can be done, and it means that you can do it too.

Your biggest win today is to allow yourself to appreciate that others' success is your success. Instead of looking at it from a position of lack like, "That is great for them but not for me," or getting into comparison mode, you can say, "If they can do it, I can do it too." Allow that to fuel you to tell your brain that you can and you will do it.

Future Thinking

Extraordinary success is understanding that what seems impossible now is only temporary. Once you discover how to embrace possibility thinking by challenging your mind to adopt new thought patterns, the opportunities are endless. When you see others achieving big things, it gives your brain proof that it's possible for you, which is modeling behavior. This is why it's important to surround yourself with people who are ahead of you or who are more experienced. I do not like to be the smartest person in the room. If I'm going to learn something new or challenging, I want to learn from others and be a sponge. I want to show my own brain that even though I might not feel successful right now, seeing others model that behavior gives me the hope, encouragement, and confidence that I can do it, too. It's just a matter of figuring out the steps to get there, just like a puzzle. When it has been done, it can be done—so let's get on with it and do it!

Think about yourself as a five-year-old. What were your likes, dislikes, and passions? I remember myself as a footloose and fancy free five-year-old. I loved to dress up in my ballet outfit, use my hairbrush like a microphone, and give the family a show every night. I would think to myself, "I'm so fabulous. My parents think I'm so fabulous." Somewhere around the age of ten I became self-conscious. I started thinking, "Oh my gosh, everyone is watching me. This is so embarrassing. I can't do this any more."

As we get older and become adults, we forget about what it feels like to just be free and embrace childlike wonder. Think about a child the night before Christmas who says, "Ooh, I'm so excited! I'm gonna open my presents tomorrow!" Just the anticipation of something great happening gets them believing. What if we as adults could tap into that wonder, that possibility, that excitement? Can you imagine the energy and the momentum you could get if you allowed yourself to start dreaming again?

You only need someone to believe with you in order for you to have the momentum, the encouragement, the energy, the thought, and the belief. Knowing that I know you can do it, because I've seen other people do it before, means it is possible for you. It's just a matter of showing you the pieces, and helping you along the way, to put one foot in front of the other. Are you ready? Let's do this!

Self-Reflection Exercise

Here are some probing questions to ask yourself:

- When did you stop believing in yourself?
- When did you lose your childlike wonder?
- Who or what disappointed you so that you stopped dreaming?

19

Critical Thinking

"Sir, my concern is not whether God is on our side; my greatest concern is to be on God's side, for God is always right."
Abraham Lincoln

Think about it: brains rule the world. It's the brains behind the people who make the decisions in business, families, government, and relationships. We go through the motions, allow circumstances to blow us into randomness. We haven't thought about what we are thinking about, so the vehicle of our life has been driving without a driver or GPS coordinates. The important thing to remember is that you are the driver of your car, the captain of your ship. You need to make sure that you are thinking correctly, so you get to where it is you want to go. Being intentional with your mind is about engaging the skill of being a critical thinker.

Disputation

Thomas Aquinas (1225-1274) was an Italian Dominican friar and priest and an influential philosopher and theologian. Aquinas was a prominent proponent of natural theology and the father of a school of thought (encompassing both theology and philosophy) known as Thomism. He argued that God is the source of the light of natural reason and the light of faith. He has been described as the most influential thinker of the medieval period, and the greatest of the medieval philosopher theologians[47]. His ideas especially influenced Western thought and modern philosophy, particularly in the areas of ethics, natural law, metaphysics, and political theory.

Disputation[48] is a word we don't hear often in twenty-first century language. In the scholastic system of education of the Middle Ages, disputations offered a formalized method of debate designed to uncover and establish truths in theology and in sciences. Fixed rules governed the process; they demanded dependence on traditional written authorities and the thorough understanding of each argument on each side.

The Merriam-Webster Dictionary defines disputation[49] as "the action of disputing, verbal controversy, an academic exercise in oral defense of a thesis by formal logic."

We find this method of thinking in today's legal system. To dispute means[50]:

> A conflict or controversy; a conflict of claims or rights; an assertion of a right, claim, or demand on one side, met by contrary claims or allegations on the other. The subject of litigation; the matter for which a suit is brought and upon which issue is joined, and in relation to which jurors are called and witnesses examined.

We find mention in the King James Bible of the word "disputation":

> *When therefore Paul and Barnabas had no small dissension and disputation with them, they determined that Paul and Barnabas, and certain other of them, should go up to Jerusalem unto the apostles and elders about this question.*
> *Acts 15:2, KJV*

> *Receive ye him that is weak in the faith, but not to judge his doubtful disputations. Romans 14:1, KJV*

What we can learn from this is that it is perfectly sound to question one's thoughts, logic, prepositions, and ideals. It is healthy to allow fair argument, analysis, and disagreement about a point of view. God gave us a brain to think; that is one of the most important aspects of our humanity. Becoming a good critical thinker requires intentional action, an open mind to hear an opposing point of view, a thorough analysis of the facts, and the humility to question one's own ego.

The Scientific Method

According to Wikipedia, the scientific method[51] is:

> An empirical method for acquiring knowledge that has characterized the development of science since at least the 17th century. It involves careful observation, applying rigorous skepticism about what is observed, given that cognitive assumptions can distort how one interprets the observation.

The scientific method is applied broadly in science and across many different fields. It involves the process of observing, asking questions, and seeking answers through tests and experiments. How the scientific method is applied is: a researcher develops a hypothesis (or idea), then tests it through various means. The idea is to find the truth by questioning and testing an idea. The outcome is not predetermined through biases, but on the basis of the outcome of the tests and experiments. The modified hypothesis is then retested, modified, and tested again. The goal is to come to a conclusion through consistency by observing phenomena and testing outcomes.

When we think of science we think in terms of absolutes, but science itself is not an absolute. It's the quest for truth by testing an idea against many different scenarios. This is why in the scientific community a scientist does not declare their findings as an absolute until it is put forward for peer review and thoroughly questioned and tested. This process of questioning the validity and truth of a concept is an important part in seeking truth. Science, as we know, is always evolving and changing as more discoveries are made each day.

The scientific method is a great problem-solving approach and has five basic steps, plus one feedback step:

- Make an observation.
- Ask a question.
- Form a hypothesis, or testable explanation.
- Make a prediction based on the hypothesis.
- Test the prediction.
- Iterate: use the results to make new hypotheses or predictions.

Therefore, what we can learn is that applying a scientific method to questioning the validity of one's own thoughts and feelings is a perfectly sound approach to developing emotional and mental maturity. Asking, "Why am I thinking or feeling this?" is a great place to start. God gave you a brain to think, so you can become a clear critical thinker who is not swayed by emotions.

Analysis Paralysis

Psychologist Barry Schwartz coined the phrase "analysis paralysis" in his book the *Paradox of Choice*: Why More Is Less to describe his consistent findings. It shows that while we think having more choices allows us to achieve better results, it also leads to greater anxiety, paralysis, indecision, and dissatisfaction. Known as "decision fatigue," too many choices cause our brains to shut down so that we prefer not to choose at all. In his 2005 TED Talk, Barry Schwartz says, "Even if you overcome the paralysis and make a choice, we end up less satisfied with the result of the choice than we would be if we had fewer options."

Rather than empowering us to make better choices, our unlimited access to more information and choices actually leads us to fear making the wrong decision. This in turn leads to us spinning our wheels in indecision, stuck in the prison of analysis paralysis. Overthinking paralyzes your productivity, makes you less happy, weakens your willpower, and kills creativity. Schwartz also says choices make people miserable because they lead to regret and anticipated regret, opportunity costs, escalation of expectations, and self-blame. Expensive, complicated choices don't help us; they actually hurt us.

Your brain is like a computer. If you have too much input, your confused mind will say no. When presented with too many options, our brains can't decide. So what does your brain do? It shuts down to preserve energy. Your brain has had to process so much input in a short amount of time, that the pressure to decide causes anxiety. It creates internal conflict when trying to weigh up the options, and the fear of missing out on the perfect choice kicks in.

You've probably experienced this when trying to order food at a restaurant. Presented with too many options, your head spins in indecision. But walk into a McDonald's or a Burger King and what you're presented with are bundled options labeled as meal 1, 2, 3, etc. By bundling a burger with fries and a drink, you now only have one choice to make and not three. That is one of the reasons why take-out food is delivered so quickly. The menu has been designed to make your decision-making easier, thereby increasing profits for the restaurant by churning out more customers.

If you've ever gone to a flea market, you will see an abundance of different options. Everything from candles, to clothing, to a florist, to a butcher. Choices, choices, choices. So how do you choose? Frankly, it's exhausting!

If you've walked past a Cartier or Tiffany store, have you noticed the display in the window? You will see a simply presented, gorgeous piece of jewelry. They have a single ring or a watch nicely laying on a clean background. That single item takes center stage, and there are no other options to sway your decision. They don't want you to compare that with the other products next door. They are painting a picture of beauty that oozes luxury and quality. Can you imagine how you're going to feel wearing this beautiful piece? They've eliminated the choices. Your brain is transfixed with a lovely item, and all you have to choose is to say yes or no. The key to critical thinking is cultivating clear and simple decision-making.

Engaging the Mind

As a modern society we are in constant consumption mode. We prefer to be passive and be entertained, or be spoon-fed facts we can spit out like a parrot. Life is meant for living, and how we find true contentment is by engaging the mind, body, and soul. Practicing presence is a lost skill we don't talk enough about.

Active listening is a learned skill that you can acquire by engaging in being present in the moment. What this means is we lean into the conversations we are having, instead of just waiting for a gap to talk.

Socrates

The Socratic method[52] of teaching is "a form of cooperative argumentative dialogue between individuals, based on asking and answering questions to stimulate critical thinking, and to draw out ideas and underlying presuppositions." Developed by the Greek philosopher Socrates in the fifth century BC, the Socratic method is a conversation between the teacher and students. The teacher poses continual probing questions in an effort to explore the underlying beliefs that shape the students' views and opinions.

> *"Do not take what I say as if I were merely playing, for you see the subject of our discussion—and on what subject should even a man of slight intelligence be more serious? —namely, what kind of life should one live . . ."*
> *Socrates*

This method of critical thinking and questioning is often lost in the modern classroom. Since the Industrial Revolution, children have been taught to absorb facts and repeat them. In my personal opinion, and not only because I'm half Greek, I believe the Greek Socratic method is a very undervalued form of assessing comprehension. How do we know if the student has absorbed any of the content if they are not given the chance to voice their opinions and explain their thinking? I believe learning happens when we lean into critical thinking and engage in an open and unbiased two-way conversation. You are not a parrot, and God gave you a brain for a reason. He also gave you two ears and one mouth, so you should listen twice as much as you speak! Asking "Why?" is a very powerful question that we should encourage to really engage the mind.

You will soon discover that within a group dynamic, people will start to learn from each other. By having a roundtable discussion, everyone is given the opportunity to talk it out. Asking "What came up for you?" is a great conversation starter. Susie might say one thing and Pam might say another, and maybe their opinions differ, but that is okay (no judgment allowed). You can give one recipe to two different chefs, and they will bake two different cakes.

We need to foster creative conversation. If we took away criticism and judgment and allowed everyone a right to their opinion, imagine what creativity we could explore! Let's learn to lean in and listen. What you have to say might enlighten me about something I've never thought of before. Our greatest aha moments and moments of development are when we have the attitude of being teachable.

Self-Reflection Exercise

You can do this with a group of friends or peers. Gather in smaller groups of between five to twelve. People feel safer sharing in an encouraging environment. Who really liked being called on in class when you were a kid? Nobody likes being put on the spot or being criticized publicly. We don't need to add layers of shame or blame to an already fragile mind. I prefer more of a roundtable discussion. We are going to learn a topic and then we are going to work through it together. Ask questions like:

· What are you thinking?
· What did you learn?
· What came up for you?

20

Intentional Change

"Without continual growth and progress, such words as improvement, achievement, and success have no meaning."
Benjamin Franklin

How many times have you tried to make changes only to find yourself slipping back into old habits? No matter whether you're trying to change a behavior, an attitude, or your current circumstances, change is never easy. The process is likely to be more like "stop, start, stop, start, stop" than a smooth transition. Inevitably your willpower fades, the desire wears off, and other priorities compete for your attention. Change is especially tough if you're trying to make a change that you don't really want to make. It's also tough if you are not fully convinced of the idea, or if you're making a change that was designed for someone else if it doesn't fully align with your goals. This is why it's helpful to create a personalized action plan.

Richard Boyatzis, is a distinguished university professor at Case Western Reserve University and adjunct professor at the International ESADE Business School. He is the co-author of the books *Primal Leadership*, *Resonant Leadership*, *Becoming a Resonant Leader,* and *Helping People Change.* He developed "Intentional Change Theory" (ICT) as part of his work on individual and organizational change. Intentional change has become a fundamental principle in psychology and management science. He published his theory in 2006 in the Journal of Management Development.

I had the delightful opportunity to personally interview Professor Boyatzis over Zoom, and he shared insightful tools. During our conversation he said;

> I think the crucial issue of today, which is why your theme (of getting unstuck) is so important, what many of us were saying back in the fall of 2020 was the real pain. Unless you've lost a close family member from Covid, the real cost was going to be the long-term mental health cost. That's what we're seeing now. We're seeing almost everybody's level of neurosis amped up. The amount of cocooning, the amount of people not wanting to go outside their homes, the amount of people just sticking with what feels safer or more comfortable, means the glue is no longer Elmers, now it's epoxy.

We literally have become stuck in our ways! Now more than ever it has become crucial that we take the steps to initiate change in our lives, or the epoxy of fear and resistance to change will become increasingly difficult to shift.

Professor Boyatzis goes on to say: "The body and mind is very amenable to change, but it has to be somewhat intentional and the right change, not just any change or us simply looking for more stimulation."

Benefits of Boredom

Many parents would agree that the effects that the lock down had on our children is noticeable. However, what it did do was give many parents (myself included) an eye-opening view into how our children prefer to be entertained. It is easy to hand them an iPad to prevent their boredom, but what we forget is that boredom can be good for a child's learning.

During our Zoom conversation, Professor Boyatzis went on to say:

We have to do a better job of asking little kids, including four and five year olds, why? They ask us why, so we have to ask them why back. We also have to do a better job of not scheduling children so much. Most children today don't have time to get bored. What bored meant years ago, whether it was after school or on a weekend or in the summer, being bored meant you had to invent a game or a toy. Right now, between tennis lessons and French lessons and all the rest of it, we over-structure our kids' time. What those things do is they give us stimulation. We think we're interacting with other's, but we're not really, because we're not working with each others emotions. By giving our children the easy thing to do and eliminating boredom, we're actually denying them the ability to learn how to build and maintain better relationships.

If we want to position ourselves and our children for a successful future and successful relationships, it's critical we embrace the skill of looking inward and being intentional to enact real change.

Intentional Change Theory

According to Professor Boyatzis:

ICT is a fractal theory. It describes why and how sustained, desired change operates at all levels, from individual to dyads, to teams to organizations to communities, to country level change. It is one of its unique features as compared to other theories of change. You treat it as individual change.

The Intentional Change theory outlines five common sense steps that you need to follow if you want to make a lasting change within yourself. These five steps are from R.E. Boyatzis' 2006 article "An Overview of Intentional Change From a Complexity Perspective," in the Journal of Management Development,

Vol. 25, No. 7:

- Discover your ideal self.
- Discover your real self.
- Create your learning agenda.
- Experiment with and practice new habits.
- Get support.

Intentional change involves: (a) envisioning the ideal self (who you wish to be and what you want to do in your work and life); (b) exploring the real self (the gaps you need to fill and the strengths that will help you make the change); (c) developing a learning agenda (a road map for turning aspirations into reality); (d) experimenting and practicing the new behaviors; and (e) creation and maintenance of caring, resonant relationships.

We want to explore a person's individual vision. Professor Boyatzis explains a useful exercise:

> Think about your whole life, not just your work, personal life or dreams. Write down the names of the people that come to mind when you answer this question, "Who helped me the most in my life to become who I am or get to where I am today?" Next to their name, jot down the words or phrases that help you remember a moment that you learned something from them. What did they say or do? How were you feeling? How does it feel having remembered these people and your relationship to them? What important thing have you remembered from this moment?

Common answers to these include: Loved. Calm. Grateful. Humbled. Warm. Strong. Safe. Appreciative. Gratitude. Supported. Playful. Relieved. Happy. Seen and heard. Valued. Connected. Encouraged. Empowered. Inspired. Tingly. Held. Thankful. Lucky. Whole. Confident. Trusting. Challenged. Alive. Open-hearted. Yearning. Delight. Treasured. Important. Uplifted. Free. Blessed. Acknowledged. Teary-eyed. Nostalgic.

People talk about feeling loved, reflect, grateful, proud, and loved. They felt appreciated, supported, seen, and heard. If you just had any of those feelings too, you just spent a few minutes renewing your parasympathetic nervous system.

Cultivating somatic awareness is developing awareness of what your body is doing. This is part of your body's renewal system. Often we confuse actual renewal with things like relaxing, resting, and boredom. But those are emotional states, not active renewal. We need to experience a light bulb moment when awareness of your emotional and mental states pops into your consciousness. This is necessary for the change to evolve. Asking the question, "What would you love your life to be like?" is not a goal but a vision. It's a dream and gives you a sense of purpose.

In the study, Professor Boyatzis found that 80 percent of the stories of people who helped you the most address your vision/dream, or possibilities, and/or strengths. These were conversations that opened you up to new possibilities. They believed in your dreams, potential, and strengths. They opened your eyes to opportunities that you didn't think you were ready for. By asking this meaningful question, it pulls out what you might consider or haven't yet, but believe is possible.

> *"If you don't have a personal vision or deep sense of purpose, there's about a 5% chance you'll make it to the second stage."*
> *Richard Boyatzis*

The ICT Stages

Discover Your Ideal Self

The first phase of intentional change is what Professor Boyatzis calls your "ideal self." In order to sustain a desired change, we need to engage in a vision of the future we want to see for ourselves. This states that:

> Change is not linear or normally distributed, and it's certainly not continuous. Change actually happens in fits and starts. It's a property called discontinuity. If you don't have a personal vision or deep sense of purpose, there's about a 5% chance you'll make it to the second stage.

It's the feeling of taking two steps forward and then one step back. You are still making progress if you just keep taking steps.

Discover Your Real Self

The second phase of intentional change is where you start to understand how you come across to others, and how others see you. Boyatzis calls it the "real self." It's not what you think of yourself, but how other people experience you. You make a comparison and come up with a personal balance sheet of strengths and weaknesses. This requires complete honesty and transparency. How do I show up for others? How am I perceived? Often this is where we are challenged to look past the masks we wear to uncover the "real self".

Create Your Learning Agenda

The third discovery is what you would love to work on. It's not a performance improvement plan. It's what Boyatzis calls the "ought self." It should not be about what you "should" or "ought" to do. It's something that you are joyfully excited about. Time to ditch the shouldas, wouldas and couldas! Think about what the steps might be that will help you move forward to your ideal goal and future self.

Experiment with and Practice New Habits

The fourth discovery is the moments of experimenting and eventually practicing new thoughts, feelings, and behaviors. At first it can feel strange and out of your comfort zone. But that is the point: to push you past the safe and steady toward your stretch goals.

Get Support

The fifth discovery is about cultivating trusting, resonant relationships to help you stay on track. We all need accountability to get things done and having a friend, coach, counselor, or colleague can provide the necessary support to keep you from giving up when it gets hard.

Positive Emotional Attractor

When people change in sustainable ways, they are pulled to an intrinsic attractor inside of them like an internal compass. Boyatzis calls it a "positive emotional attractor." He contends that inside each of us and in each of our relationships, teams, organizations, communities, and countries, we have a positive and a negative emotional attractor. The positive emotional attractor is something that activates the parasympathetic nervous system, your body's neurohormonal system. When you engage your "positive emotional attractor," you are activating the renewal process, whereas the "negative emotional attractor," which is the analytic network, activates the stress response.

> *"Being in the positive emotional attractor versus the negative emotional attractor is the difference between thinking of possibilities versus problems, dreams versus expectations, optimism versus pessimism."*
> Dr. Richard Boyatzis

The reason this is so powerful is that it is the difference between hope and fear. Thinking about your strengths versus your weaknesses makes you excited about trying something new, versus obligations or things you feel you "should" do. We need to start in the positive emotional attractor by outlining our dreams and visions. This positive energy will help drive you to reach beyond your current circumstances.

Negative Emotional Attractor

Think of your decisions about what to study, where to live, and where to work, and whether they might have been influenced by your positive or negative emotional attractors. If they include the "shoulda, woulda, coulda" decisions, my guess is they are on the negative side. Did you choose that avenue of study because Mom and Dad thought it was a good idea? Or maybe you felt that you didn't want to disappoint them? If you are fully invested in the idea, then you will be motivated by your positive emotional attractor to keep going. Whereas if the decision was made out of fear, that negative emotional attractor will keep you stuck in oughts or shoulds.

If you start in the negative emotional attractor, you go into the stress response and you start to close down, cognitively, perceptually, and emotionally. The negative emotional attractor is a defensive posture, and you literally start to cocoon. That is why treatment adherence is so abysmal in healthcare. People do about 50 percent of what their physician or nurse tells them to do to get over a disease or surgery. If you start the effort by focusing on a problem, you've just killed the change effort. So telling patients that smoking kills is not the best way to motivate them to stop smoking. They need to buy into the idea of why not smoking has much more health benefits, so they can be internally motivated to succeed.

Humans need both the negative emotional attractor and positive emotional attractor. Just like the idiom called "the carrot or the stick". It is an [53] incentivization method in which a reward and a punishment are simultaneously offered/threatened as a motivation to complete some task.

We need the negative emotional attractor to help us solve problems, but we can't live our lives in fear in a defensive posture. The positive emotional attractor is phenomenal, but can cause inaction and a happy-go-lucky attitude where nothing gets done. To create some semblance of a balance, we have to over-sample the positive emotional attractor.

The Positive to Negative Ratio

Barbara L. Fredrickson, Ph.D., earned her doctorate from Stanford University. Fredrickson's foundational research led her to develop a theory on positive emotions called "Broaden and Build Theory." The substance of this theory is that positive emotions play an essential role in our survival. Positive emotions, like love, joy, and gratitude promote new and creative actions, ideas, and social bonds. When people experience positive emotions, their minds broaden, and they open up to new possibilities and ideas.

The theory also suggests that negative emotions serve the opposite function of positive ones. When threatened with negative emotions like anxiety, fear, frustration, or anger, the mind constricts and focuses on the imposing threat (whether real or imagined). This in turn limits one's ability to be open to new ideas and to build resources and relationships. In her 2009 book, Positivity[54], Fredrickson's research defines positivity and how it can transform people's lives. Her research showed that an approximate three to one ratio of positivity was the ideal. Experiencing three to one positive emotions to negative emotions leads people to achieve optimal levels of well-being and resilience. Fredrickson concludes that a positive state of mind can enhance relationships, improve health, relieve depression, and broaden the mind.

Blind Spots

Nobody likes the feeling of being stuck. Sometimes we need somebody else to help us see what we are not seeing, because we all have blind spots. The whole point is to put your defenses down and to be really honest with yourself. If you're not getting results and the transformation that you seek, let's figure out why. Let's peel back the layers and remove the masks. Go slow to go fast to figure out how to get yourself moving by taking baby steps.

Being open to feedback is critical for growth. What did you learn about that? What are your 'Ahas'? What's the one thing you're going to do with what you learned? What's the one takeaway you're going to implement over the next week, or month, or year? Focus on just one thing to take action on. You will gain a lot more confidence and momentum when you feel like you are achieving that one thing. So implement that one thing, and start seeing results.

It's Never Too Late

Here is some encouragement: no matter what you are thinking and dreaming or planning to do, there's always a do-over. There is always time. It's never too late. You can always hit the reset button. You can always go back to factory settings. But you first have to be aware. Be determined and be consistent enough to show up. Put one foot in front of the other, because it can be done, if you are ready and prepared to do the work of getting unstuck.

Self-Reflection Exercise

Answer these questions to help you broaden your viewpoint and expand your thinking to invite the positive emotional attractor to engage.

- If your life were absolutely perfect ten to fifteen years from now, what would it be like?
- What kind of person do you want to be when others interact with you?
- What are your core values that are most important to you?

21

Dreaming & Visioneering

"Then the LORD replied; "Write down the revelation and make it plain on tablets so that a herald may run with it."
Habakkuk 2:2, NIV

Do you have the desire to escape the constant push of, "I got to do, got to do, got to do?" Do you long to escape the rat race? If you have been running on a constant loop and you don't know how to make it stop, we need to start at the end. We need to paint a picture of positivity of where you can be. My anti-mainstream method isn't about making you feel guilty about what you're missing, but instead to encourage you to dream. Think about where you want to be. Let's take the lid off your limitations. Let's think big. When you're committed to the vision, you are going to take the action.

Get into problem-solving mode about the possibilities to put you in a ownership mindset to think in terms of growth. You do have hope and agency, and being creative and curious is healthy for emotional wholeness.

There's a difference between being interested and being committed. It's like window shopping. No one actually buys from window shopping. You've got to walk in the door to make a purchase. How do we make somebody walk through the door? We've got to make the environment enticing. We've got to be positive. You've got to have the flowers to attract the bees.

When you have a purpose, mission, and goal in mind, you are not going to be swayed by the winds of change. You will know with confidence, clarity, and certainty where you are going. When temptations come to distract you, you will be fiercely grounded in pursuing the vision.

A stumbling block can be decision fatigue. If you are finding it hard to make a decision, it could be that you have too many options to choose from. A confused mind will always say no then apathy sets in.

What Is Holding You Back?

I have a question for you. What is holding you back from achieving your dreams? Do you even know what it is? Building a vision of the future is one of the most important activities you can engage in. Looking ahead to where you want to go helps to make the steps clearer of how to get there. Are you stuck in the past or the present? When you focus on your current circumstances, or look to the past for confirmation, you can't see the possibility of what could be. We don't know what we don't know. When we don't have a positive experience to rely on, we automatically assume that everything is going to remain the same.

Imagine your dream life. Too many people don't take the time to imagine what their actual dream life could look like. They think it's out of reach or too big, and then settle for mediocrity. Allowing yourself the chance to dream and to think big without restrictions, without the past to show you what could be, allows you to take off the shackles of your potential.

Allowing yourself to dream big with no restrictions of time, money, or resources allows you to really think beyond the possibilities and out of the box of what you have available to achieve. What is your dream life? What if you could have everything your heart desires? Perhaps it's a happy family with regular vacations, or a romantic relationship, or going to far away places, or being able to feel like you are fully embodying who you are, or being fit and healthy in your body, or having time for all of the above.

Sometimes we think we have to choose between a successful business, a happy family, or a healthy life. But what if you could have it all? This is totally possible when you take yourself out of the equation. Get that eagle-eye vision, and start to see the big picture so you can see the steps with your perspective.

Once you've thought it through, and you've had the vision of what it could be, your brain is given the capacity to see that it's actually possible. Then you can simply work backwards taking the incremental steps to make the path clear. So many people don't achieve big goals because they think it's so far out there. But if you take the approach of taking one step at a time, and you're constantly moving forward, you won't give up. You won't get discouraged because you just know it's part of the path.

The Power of Imagination

What is your big overall life dream? Some people like to call it their "BHAG": the big, hairy, audacious goal. What or who motivates you to keep dreaming? Is it your family? Is it a goal for the future to create a legacy? Take the time to actually think about it.

> *"Then the Lord replied, 'Write down the revelation and make it plain on tablets so that a herald may run with it for the revelation awaits an appointed time. It speaks of the end and will not prove false. Though it linger, wait for it. It will certainly come and it'll not delay.'"*
> *Habakkuk 2:2-3, NIV*

When we partner with God, He gives us a vision, and we need to write it down. With His direction we can see the steps. Our responsibility is to put faith into action by putting our boots on the ground to make things happen. When God gives you a vision, He will give you the people, the process, and the potential to be able to fulfill the vision and He will give everything you need. It first starts with us imagining the possibility and writing it down.

Dreaming Reflection Exercise

Make the time to dream. Set aside maybe one to two hours when your brain is fresh and you don't have any immediate commitments. You don't have to go anywhere. There's no pressing appointments or phone calls or texts or emails. It's important not to rush the process. You want to remove any distractions. Put your phone on mute and shut down your computer. Pick a neutral environment, maybe going to a coffee shop or an area where you feel more creative. The idea is to sit quietly, letting yourself dream without any limitations.

Adults tend to forget their inner child. This is an important part of the dreaming process, because when you remember yourself as a child, there are no limitations. You could think you could fly to the stars. We want to tap into that belief that anything is possible. Engage your inner child, the one who could stare at the clouds all day, and let yourself dream. Engage your innermost desires, wants, and longings. Think about the dreams and the visions you haven't actually articulated yet. Maybe you haven't said them out loud or written them down, but they've been stirring in your heart for months, maybe years. Think about them in detail and how it would feel to live your dream life. Don't refer to the past or the present of what your future could be like, but really take off the shackles and think about what it feels like to be living your life, your dream life, right now.

Close your eyes and visualize the future you want. Then record it in writing. No one is watching or judging you, and this is your space to imagine what's possible for yourself. Imagine the sights, the feelings, and the environment you've created. What does your day look like? What is a day in the life of a successful person you feel like? What are you doing? Just imagine the details. The more details you can put down, the more clearer the path will become.

> *"If you fail to plan, you're planning to fail."*
> *Benjamin Franklin*

We often take for granted that we have it within our ability today to make changes. It doesn't have to be a pipe dream if we are willing to take action. Start taking those steps towards your ideal future. Benjamin Franklin is famously known for his quote, "If you fail to plan, you're planning to fail." So start with the big picture. It's easier to zoom out just like an eagle. Rise above your current situation and get an eagle-eye vision with more perspective.

Self-Reflection Exercise

Take a pen and paper, and take time to think and write about these following time frames: ten years from now, five years from now, one year from now, and ninety days from now. Sometimes it's easier to work backward from ten years to help you zoom out to see the big picture, so you can start with the bigger version and then zoom in for clarity. This will help you make it easier to understand what needs to be done and in what order, what is for now and what is for later. Do this process more than once. Over time it becomes useful because you can look back and see that your goals and visions were. They might change as you start to see that they are achievable. The important part is that this process will help you break down the steps to make your dreams achievable. Once you know the steps to take, you simply need to go out and execute them. Now, remember: there are no wrong or right answers. You can do this, I believe in you!

- What do you need to change today to make your dreams and visions a reality?
- So what are you waiting for?

Use the guided questions in the study guide to help you develop a clear vision: https://www.mimikacooney.com/unstick

Take this process further by joining my 12 step Unstick Your Mind program: https://www.unstickyourmind.com

Extra Offers

Complimentary Gift

www.mimikacooney.com/unstick

Review

As an author, it is important to get **reviews** from valuable readers like you so that future readers can make better decisions. Your opinion is important and I truly value your feedback. Please help me by leaving your honest review on your preferred bookstores thank you!

More Books

If you enjoyed this book, check out other books in my collection:
Book Collection www.mimikacooney.com/books
Unstick Your Mind www.mimikacooney.com/unstick
Mindset Make Over www.mimikacooney.com/mindset
Worrier to Warrior www.mimikacooney.com/warrior
Power Prayers www.mimikacooney.com/powerprayers
Unlock the Mind of a Champion www.mimikacooney.com/champion
Anxiety Anonymous www.mimikacooney.com/anxiety

Share

If you enjoyed this book and found the content useful, please share it with your friends. Please tag me @mimikacooney and use the hashtag #UnstickYourMind so I can thank you.

Enroll in the Program

https://www.unstickyourmind.com

More Free Resources

https://www.mimikacooney.com

Join our Book Launch Team

If you enjoy reading and reviewing books and free giveaways, come join my book launch team:
https://mimikacooney.com/launchteam

Connect with me Online

Website https://www.mimikacooney.com
YouTube https://youtube.com/c/mimikacooney
LinkedIn https://www.linkedin.com/in/mimikacooney
Facebook https://www.facebook.com/themimikacooney
Instagram https://www.instagram.com/mimikacooney
Twitter https://twitter.com/mimikacooney
Pinterest https://www.pinterest.com/mimikacooney
Rumble https://rumble.com/c/MimikaTV

Notes

WHY MINDSET IS EVERYTHING

1   https://www.google.com/search?client=firefox-b-1-d&q=define+neuroplasticity

2   https://www.merriam-webster.com/dictionary/metacognition

3   https://metacognition.is-fabulous.com

4   https://danielamenmd.com

5   https://drleaf.com/blogs/news/why-we-keep-making-the-same-mistakes-tips-to-break
-bad-habits

6   https://www.sciencedaily.com/releases/2021/03/210303091405.htm

POWER OF AWARENESS

7   https://positivepsychology.com/false-beliefs/

WHAT IS YOUR STUCK STORY?

8   https://en.wikipedia.org/wiki/Outliers_(book)

9   https://www.ncbi.nlm.nih.gov/pmc/articles/PMC4662388

10 https://newsroom.ucla.edu/releases/Putting-Feelings-Into-Words-Produces-8047

11 https://self-compassion.org

THE TODDLER, TEENAGER, & THERAPIST

12 https://en.wikipedia.org/wiki/Hedonic_treadmill

13 https://brenebrown.com

SLOW DOWN TO SPEED UP

14 https://www.amenclinics.com

15 https://drleaf.com

16 https://www.psychologytoday.com/us/blog/out-the-ooze/201611/the-perils-social-isolati
on

THE EMOTIONAL ROLLER COASTER

17 https://lisafeldmanbarrett.com

18 https://www.ted.com/talks/lisa_feldman_barrett_you_aren_t_at_the_mercy_of_your
_emotions_your_brain_creates_them

19 https://complete-coherence.com/team/dr-alan-watkins

20 https://joyely.com/

DONE IS BETTER THAN PERFECT

21 https://copyblogger.com/open-loops/

POWER OF WORDS

22 https://thewellnessenterprise.com/emoto

23 http://www.andrewnewberg.com/books/how-god-changes-your-brain-breakthrough-findings-from-a-leading-neuroscientist

HABIT REINVENTION

24 https://drleaf.com/blogs/news/why-we-keep-making-the-same-mistakes-tips-to-break-bad-habits

25 https://en.wikipedia.org/wiki/Kaizen

PIVOT, ADAPT, OPPORTUNITY

26 https://poultry.extension.org/articles/poultry behavior/normal-behaviors-of-chickens-in-small-and-backyard-poultry-flocks

27 https://thehensloft.com/chicken-body-language

28 https://www.eagles.org/what-we-do/educate/learn-about-eagles/bald-eagle-behavior

29 https://www.britannica.com/animal/eagle-bird

30 https://animalbehaviorcorner.com/behavior-of-bald-eagle

CHALLENGING LIMITING BELIEFS

31 https://www.danielplan.com/dr-amen-use-your-brain-to-change-your-age-2

32 https://drleaf.com/blogs/news/you-are-not-a-victim-of-your-biology

33 https://en.wikipedia.org/wiki/Five_whys

STOP THE SELF-SABOTAGE

34 https://depts.washington.edu/uwbrtc/our-team/marsha-linehan

35 https://my.clevelandclinic.org/health/treatments/22838-dialectical-behavior-therapy-dbt

FIXED VERSUS GROWTH MINDSET

36 https://profiles.stanford.edu/carol-dweck

37 https://www.goodreads.com/book/show/40745.Mindset

38 https://fs.blog/carol-dweck-mindset/

FIXED TO FLEXIBILITY

39 https://psychology.osu.edu/people/crocker.37

PUSHING THROUGH BOUNDARIES

40 https://www.nicabm.com/program/stuck

41 https://pubmed.ncbi.nlm.nih.gov/19398384

42 https://www.psychologytoday.com/us/therapy-types/acceptance-and-commitment-therapy

43 https://www.psychologytoday.com/us/blog/get-out-your-mind/200901/human-life-is-not-problem-be-solved

44 https://www.psychologytoday.com/us/therapy-types/acceptance-and-commitment-therapy

45 https://www.nicabm.com/program/trauma-siegel

UNLOCK POSSIBILITY THINKING

46 https://en.wikipedia.org/wiki/Roger_Bannister

CRITICAL THINKING

47 Chenu, Marie-Dominique. "St. Thomas Aquinas". *Encyclopedia Britannica*, Invalid Date, https://www.britannica.com/biography/Saint-Thomas-Aquinas. Accessed 13 April 2023.

48 https://en.wikipedia.org/wiki/Disputation

49 https://www.merriam-webster.com/dictionary/disputation

50 https://legal-dictionary.thefreedictionary.com/dispute

51 https://en.wikipedia.org/wiki/Scientific_method

52 https://en.wikipedia.org/wiki/Socratic_method

INTENTIONAL CHANGE

53 https://idioms.thefreedictionary.com/the+carrot+or+the+stick

54 https://www.goodreads.com/book/show/5629833-positivity

About the Author

Mimika Cooney is a leading faith-based Christian mindset author and speaker known as the "Personal Trainer for Your Mind." She empowers ambitious Christians to rewire their brain by combining neuroscience, positive psychology, and a faith-based approach. Mimika will teach you how to unstick your mind, develop emotional resilience, and unlock high performance by becoming the boss of your brain! She loves to empower purpose-driven individuals to transform their lives by shifting their mindset habits and patterns, as they pursue growth to achieve extraordinary results. She is the creator of the "Unstick Your Mind" mindset mastery method, a transformative program that equips Christians with the tools to achieve their breakthroughs.

After experiencing severe rejection, bullying, and a broken childhood, Mimika spent years seeking accolades, addicted to approval in the pursuit of finding her worth, validation, and confidence through chasing achievements. Then God stepped in to heal her hurts, change her heart, and awaken a passion for helping others seeking their own purpose in life. Mimika is passionate about empowering and equipping others to fulfill their God given purpose by sharing the message of God's grace with a world lost in negativity.

Mimika is an empowering motivational speaker, author of ten published books, twenty-five-year entrepreneur, international award-winning photographer, and veteran podcast host of the *Mimika TV* show. *Huffington Post* nominated her as one of "50 Women Entrepreneurs to Follow in 2017." *Podcasting Magazine* nominated Mimika among the "Top 50 Moms in Podcasting" in 2020.

Mimika is a native of South Africa and citizen of the USA and England. She has been married to her childhood sweetheart since 1996, and they have three children together. She is a ferocious reader and avid writer. When she is not dreaming up creative concepts, speaking, writing books, or hosting her podcast, she will be found perfecting her spins on the ice as a competitive adult figure skater. As a personal challenge, Mimika took up skating as an adult at age thirty-one. She has made it her mission to retrain her brain and muscle memory to learn this new skill. She has gone on to win several skating medals, which goes to show that you can teach an old dog new tricks!

You can connect with me on:

🌐 https://www.mimikacooney.com
🐦 https://twitter.com/mimikacooney
📘 https://www.facebook.com/themimikacooney
🔗 https://www.unstickyourmind.com
🔗 https://youtube.com/c/mimikacooney
🔗 https://www.instagram.com/mimikacooney
🔗 https://amazon.com/author/mimikacooney
🔗 https://www.linkedin.com/in/mimikacooney
🔗 https://rumble.com/MimikaTV
🔗 https://www.tiktok.com/@mimikacooney

Subscribe to my newsletter:

✉ https://www.mimikacooney.com/unstick

Also by Mimika Cooney

See Mimika's Book Collection:
https://www.mimikacooney.com/books

Mindset Make Over: How to Renew your Mind and Walk in God's Authority
https://www.mimikacooney.com/mindset
Do you feel worried, afraid, anxious, doubtful, angry, depressed, confused? Do you know God is calling you to greatness but you feel far from great? If you are ready to ditch the excuses and take back your authority as a child of God then this book is for you! Recognize damaging thoughts and stop them from influencing your life. Gain control over your mind to find freedom, peace and clarity so you are not swayed by daily stress. Use these strategies so you can become immovable when dealing with life's challenges.

Unstick Your Mind: Shift Your Mindset, Develop Grit & Break Barriers
https://www.mimikacooney.com/unstick
Are you ready to change your life by changing your mind? Every problem in life starts with a thought. Often we get stuck in perpetual cycles of bad thought patterns that cause us to repeat behaviors over and over again. Once you learn how to shift your mindset and develop grit, you will be positioned to break through any barrier holding you back! You may think its is a pipe dream but it is reality based on the concept of Neuroplasticity. The brain is an amazing organ that is always learning. The good news is that you are not stuck with the brain you have! You CAN learn new ways, new habits, and new success driven behaviors to finally achieve your goals.

Unlock the Mind of a Champion: How Ordinary People Achieve the Extraordinary

https://www.mimikacooney.com/champion

How do seemingly ordinary people achieve the extraordinary? Do they possess a special secret that the rest of us are not aware of in their achievement of personal success? In this growth mindset book you will discover the keys used by elite athletes, entrepreneurs, high achievers and inspirational bible figures that enabled them to outperform mediocrity. Come along a journey of self discovery to learn the strategies, steps, tips, tools and mindset for success that you can implement to achieve your goals and dreams.

Anxiety Anonymous: Flipping the Script on the Fear that keeps you Stuck

https://www.mimikacooney.com/anxiety

It's time to flip the script on the fear, the stress and anxiety that keeps you stuck! Anxiety is that nagging feeling that stops you from achieving your ambitions. Discover the root of anxiety, why it can sometimes be good for you, and how to leverage this strong emotion to turn it into fuel for action. Get ready to switch your brain into achievement mode, and adopt a mindset for success, as you ditch the drama queen in your mind!

Worrier to Warrior: A Mother's Journey from Fear to Faith

https://www.mimikacooney.com/warrior

This is a powerful spiritual warfare manual for women seeking empowerment. "Worrier to Warrior" is a true story of one mother's harsh reality of struggling through grief, depression, suicide, burnout, failure, anxiety and lost hope. You're in the middle of spiritual warfare with an unseen enemy. He is wreaking havoc in your home, family, and life. As a Christian woman living in a modern world, you need effective tools to fight your battles and win. The insights shared in this book will give you a battle plan you need to create a life outside of worry so you can become the undefeated royal warrior princess that you are! Break free from the mental prison that keeps you in dark places and thrives in the light of God's Word so you can become the warrior you are meant to be!

Power Prayers & Proclamations

https://www.mimikacooney.com/powerprayers

This powerful prayers and proclamations book will help refresh your daily devotional time, as a handy reference for whenever you need to deepen your walk with God. We all sin, and just like taking a daily shower, these prayers are a spiritual shower. Designed as a prayer notebook for women, it is a perfect pairing with your bible as a prayer journal for Christians. Step into your spiritual authority and watch God move in your life in miraculous ways!

Made in the USA
Columbia, SC
22 April 2024

34467828R00104